A Window on My Life

Short Autobiographical Accounts

Edited by Julia Waring
Cover by Ian Tyrrell

Dreamcatcher Publishing Limited

Memory Catcher®
A Window on My Life

Published in Great Britain by
Dreamcatcher Publishing Limited

This edition published in 2007
ISBN 0955499208
9780955499203

Dreamcatcher Publishing Limited
The School House
Bardfield Road, Thaxted, Dunmow
Essex CM6 2LW
Tel: 01371 831087

Limited Company Number: 4463969

British Library Cataloguing in Publication Data.
A CIP catalogue record for this book is available from the
British Library.

Printed and bound in Great Britain by RPM Print & Design,
Chichester, West Sussex.

Editor's Note
& Acknowledgements

The wonderful autobiographical accounts in this book have been written by a group of writers from across Essex and are the result of the first ever Memory Catcher scheme run in partnership with Essex County Council.

I hope you enjoy reading these accounts as much as I have! In addition to finding it difficult to stop reading, I found myself deeply humbled by so many of the life experiences these writers have had. One common thread between all of the accounts is the humour with which these writers have often taken extremely hard experiences which I find absolutely incredible at times. As I read on, I was forced to question whether I would have had the same strength of character in the same situations.

In addition to the writers themselves, I would like to thank Essex County Council for supporting us on this pilot project and particular thanks must go to Anne Brimlow, Malcolm Burgess, Will Chaney, Mark Curteis, Duncan Manson, Gerry Moore, Stephanie Moore, Jill Shakespear and Olivia Walley. This book would not be here without them.

Julia Waring
Editor

Contents

First Years By Mo Brannigan. 11

Alice Street, Tidal Basin, E16 By Patricia Butcher. 21

A Continental Holiday By Dorene Carr. 25

Marni By Meg Hinds. 33

An Autobiographical Sketch By Derek Maldon Fitch. 41

Social Work Stories – an excerpt By Charles Middleton 47

What Did You Do In The War Grandad?
By Charles Middleton. 59

Pictures In My Mind By Molly Middleton 67

To My Mother By Margaret O'Regan 79

A Small Boy Goes To War By Ben Paterson. 87

Holiday Job By Arthur Razzell 97

A Thirties Christmas And Beyond By Primrose Razzell. 105

A Wren In The Rigging By Jo Robson. 117

Precious Moments By Pat Sizer. 133

Knocking Off The Corners (an excerpt from a full autobiography)
By Len Stephenson 143

Brownie Camp By Jan Baldwin 151

Contents

Marie and John *By Marie Carr* 155

The 'Old Girls' Return To St. Joseph's, Kalim Pong
By Ivor Cleverley 159

About A Child *By Beryl Dore* 163

First Love *By Beryl Dore* 167

Memories Caught *By John Gibbs* 173

September 1939 *By Joyce Hunter* 179

Childhood Memories *By Hilda Miley* 183

Foggy Memories *By Michael Robertson* 197

War Years Memories *By Jean Moore* 201

Memories Of Our Young Lives *By Grace Overall* 209

My First Memory Of The Second World War
By Doreen Petitt 215

First Atlantic Crossing *By Dave Price* 219

Anyone For Country Dancing? *By Alan Sharp* 225

Memories *By Alice Smith* 229

Pathfinders *By June Smith* 231

My Memories As A Child Of Eleven In 1939
By Betty Sommerville 235

Contents

King George V And Queen Mary's Silver Jubilee, 1935
By Fred Spence *241*

No Regrets By Joan Stevens *245*

An Autobiographical Account By Doris Stone *251*

The Life And Times Of Sally Young (an excerpt from her
full autobiography) By Sally Young *255*

The Corridors of Power By Doug Powell *263*

Wartime Memories Of A Gordon Highlander
By Malcolm McCallum. *271*

As I Remember By Don Taylor *283*

The Evacuees By Don MacKenzie. *287*

My Life Story By Peggy Miller *293*

First Years

By Mo Brannigan

Today is a Bank Holiday but, looking back, I cannot remember any Bank Holidays when I was young except for Christmas. Weekends were different because we wore "Sunday" clothes and went to Church and, very occasionally, Dad took us for a drive to Epping Forest. We belonged to the lucky few who owned a car as my father was a doctor.

My father was one of six children who lived in a village outside Cork. He grew up on a farm that is still in the family but is much smaller now. My brother and I stayed there when war first broke out and found the freedom, after town life, to be liberating. Our great delight was a shallow stream that flowed alongside the house, complete with stepping stones. Did we get wet that often? I cannot remember!

The farmhouse was also the village shop, complete with drawers and jars full of sugar, tea, flour, biscuits, tobacco, matches and all manner of interesting things. At night the counter became the pub bar and the locals came in for their beer and spirits. Children were not allowed in but we would linger as we passed through from the upstairs family rooms to the outside kitchen. There was no electricity and lamps hung giving a gentle light to a room yellow with years of smoking. Neither was there running water - that came from the stream or from a pump up the lane.

My father qualified in the 1920s and came to London with two good friends. After many locums, each married and bought a practice and house in East London; the Stratford/Leytonstone area. The house my parents purchased was a large Victorian building. At some time in its past it had been a shop - we never could completely erase the marks the shelves had made in what I remember as our dining room. The dining room was semi basement as was the kitchen and scullery. The best rooms in the house became the surgery and waiting room though originally they must have been the dining room and lounge.

A flight of steps led up to the front doors complete with jardiniers of geraniums. I can still see them if I get the scent on my hands. There were two doors so that the surgery was cut off from the house when open. Patients could go directly into the waiting room - no receptionists or appointments in those days!

The far end of the surgery was a conservatory and this was where my dad dispensed the routine medicines. He had a bright pink mix that, looking back, was used for many complaints! Across the road from us, among the parade of shops, was a chemist. I can still see the large bottles of different colours and shapes. The chemist must have dispensed the stronger drugs making up each prescription. So different to the array of boxes of pills that we see these days at Boots! We earned pocket money by washing up the bottles and jars that were returned. A tedious job!

Before the National Health Service came in, all visits and attention from the doctors had to be paid for though sometimes it might be 'in kind'. My dad was not very good on the paperwork side and his brother would come and try and make sense of his jottings. He preferred to talk to the people who came in and it was noticeable that, if he was not working on a particular day, the surgery would be over much earlier! On these occasions, I often heard people say "I'll wait to see the real doctor."

Surgery was twice a day every day of the week except Sunday evenings but it seemed to us that my father was on call all hours. Apart from the calls that could be expected, there was plenty of variety. Births with problems - or deaths (although there was little he could do for the patient, he knew the families and could support them). He cut toenails and massaged strains but our delights were the calls to section people! The most outstanding of these was the man who lived in the middle of a terrace of two-up–two-down houses and had systematically removed every structure between the ground floor and the roof – and all done before anyone thought to check on the noises!

The whole family were responsible for taking all messages and the addresses for patient visits. Great was our delight when a roster of six doctors was formed to cover Saturday afternoons and Sundays, freeing us up.

When the war came, I was only five years old - the eldest of three - and had only just started school. My youngest brother was born in the August so I was sent to Ireland with the elder brother but we only stayed there for six months. We returned to London and stayed for the remainder of the war as Dad decided that, if he was staying in the area, then we all would. As the lowest floor of the house was semi-basement, the larder became our shelter and, if we were not sleeping on the shelves, we slept in the dining room. This became a "ward" when all three of us went down with Measles and Chickenpox.

We heard the noise of the gunfire and bombing and sometimes saw the fires of the Blitz but, in the way of all children, accepted this as a fact of life. The fires in the docks to me were spectacular. The gunfire and lights were like a firework show. I hate fireworks now and avoid all displays. If the buses were running, we went to school. If not, we brought home extra work to do at the kitchen table.

The Blitz was followed by the 'V Rocket' bombs. There were two kinds; V1s just fell and V2s cut out and drifted on before falling. When it suddenly went quiet, everyone learnt to dive in to the nearest shelter. A V2 fell behind the shops across from us and it brought down ceilings and windows. It also cleaned the chimney of all its soot for ages! We came out of the larder shelter to find this thick, sooty layer of dust over everything. My poor Mum! We children went to stay with nearby friends but my parents had to "camp out" as we had the surgery on the premises and the place had to be cleaned up Then, no sooner were some repairs done, than a second V Bomb fell a little further away causing damage again. We were not allowed a second lot of repairs with the exception of being allowed to replace the surgery windows. You were not expected to be bombed twice!

When my parents bought the house, trams ran outside and they told us how the tracks were swept clear at night to make them quieter. Later, we had trolley buses and found it exciting when the overhead lines became disconnected and a long pole was brought out from underneath to hitch the lines up again. Buses ran frequently and, after the war, it was usual to catch a bus to the end of the line, buy an ice-cream and then return home. It could not have been too expensive or we would not have been allowed to do this to fill holiday time. How many children could do this as safely nowadays??

We three children enjoyed the long hot summers. I had another girl to gang up on my brothers and there was no school and often no mum to keep us busy. We were also freed from the responsibility of being the doctor's family. We grew up in the years when the professional classes were looked up to, to set a standard. We had a nanny and there was a second live-in maid to help with the housework. We were recognised when we went out by the patients and reports would get back if observed not behaving "prim and proper" with our school hats askew, or the bigger sin of eating sweets or an ice-cream. The war changed much of this. The nanny joined up, clothes were on coupons, routines were upset and there were more important things for the grown-ups to worry about.

Food these days is always in the news with diets and recipes. The only recipes that interested the war-time mum were in the nature of substitutes and make-do ideas. Unfortunately, I remember little of those days. I can recall ice-cream made from frozen custard, the dried eggs, the marzipan made from semolina and flavouring and using carrots to sweeten cakes and puddings. We had less food for a week than is eaten in one good meal these days. It was a case of jam or spread, not both. We went to Ireland to visit relatives in 1945 and became quite ill from the richness of the food. I can still recall the taste of eating sandwiches of butter and sugar! Children did not get a tea ration but the Ministry orange juice was very welcome.

Unlike today, Health and Hygiene were not an important consideration. The shops, I remember, were open to the pavements - at least until the rationing and the bombing began. Meat, fish and vegetables were on display for all to see and handle. Our milk was delivered by a horse-drawn cart and, as the milkman had to go round the side way (no doorstop deliveries for us!), the horse would try and follow and pull the cart across the pavement and in through the gate!

The family in Ireland tried to help out and sent us a turkey for Christmas or an occasional beef joint but there was no freezing, or plastics, or a fast delivery postal service, so the smell of over-ripe meat is easily recalled to this day. The postman would gladly hand over the parcel! To this day I cannot eat boiled beef! Bread was either rationed or on allocation, even after the war ended. I recall the delight when sweets came off ration. It was a long time before we saw our first banana! I was at boarding school then and can recall one girl's horror at the taste.

Sometimes, when I think about the war years, the picture in my mind is 'wash day' - wet washing hanging to dry in the kitchen as we did school work at the table surrounded by it all. We did not have a washing machine until the

1950s and so washing spread over several days. We had a boiler built in under the draining board. It was a big tub that had a fire lit under it regardless of the day's temperature. Some clothes went into a tub and were rubbed on a corrugated glass board (the original boards had been used in the 'Skiffle' groups). There were little blue bags added to the white wash to improve the colour and always a big bowl of very hot starch for the linen and shirts. Then all the washing went through the mangle. Now that could give you muscles! Actually, Great Gran was still using hers in the 1960's much to my children's amazement. The washing then went out on the line for a good blow. On wet days it would have to hang on a Molly Maid - wooden slats that were suspended from the ceiling so that the washing could dry from the heat of the fire. Oh, the steam and drips of a wash day! The next day, everything was ironed and put back on the airer to ensure it was completely dry before it was put away. Damp clothes were to be avoided at all costs. Once the war was over, the sheets and linen went to a laundry service that took away the dirty and returned it all clean and ironed. Such a relief for every one.

The first washing machine we had was a single tub and this had an electric mangle on the top which wasn't really an advantage as smaller items would become caught up and spin round and round pinging off buttons and stretching elastic to breaking point. My mother-in-law had a machine that included a spin tub and it was very usual to find her spread-eagled trying to keep it in place so that the hose emptied into the sink and not all over the floor! I was told that this machine could double as a dish washer but imagine the disaster if the wrong button was pressed!

Keeping the house clean could not have been very easy. No light weight Hoovers and spray polishes then. We had a live-in maid for the "rough work"; a real east-ender from a local home for deserted girls who were kept on to go out on service. Her main job was to keep the surgery area clean but she also kept the steps and stairs clean and the brass polished. There was a regular routine for cleaning – a certain task on a certain day.

The three of us were expected to entertain ourselves. No TV or computers then! The radio played an important part in our lives and I think this is why we still remember the programmes and catch-words so easily now. When we were bombed out and sent to live with friends we discovered the gramophone. We had certain records that were favourites and would march and counter-march around the garden inventing complicated patterns. Now, I can only recall Flannigan and Allen's 'Underneath the Arches' but we must have worn a groove to other favourites.

Like hundreds of others we had our first television for the Coronation. The sitting room was not very big but we crowded in and watched every move. However, it was several years before it surplanted the radio as transmitting hours were limited.

When the war ended, my brothers and I started a new regime. We went away to boarding school. The decision was made when my eldest brother's health became a problem. He had to go to secondary school by steam train but these trains were unreliable and affected by the constant fogs and smog of one particularly bad winter. He had been prone to

18

chest infections since birth so the decision was made to send both brothers to a school in the country specialising in farm foods. Ironically, the site is now in a built-up area near to Heathrow! I went to the coast of Kent with another daughter of a doctor.

I welcomed boarding school having been an avid reader of school stories but it wasn't like the stories at all! My overwhelming feeling was the cold. We slept in big dormitories and the windows were always open except on foggy nights. No heating or duvets in those days – and having a bath was a real penance! All this was an accepted way of life though. We also went swimming in the sea in the summer months, regardless of the temperature. However, it was not all misery as there were many good times. Many of the girls came from France and Belgium and, although we did not have language classes, we all developed a good ear to follow the conversations. The school was run on a system of family units with the older ones taking care of the younger ones at all times except during lessons.

The order of nuns were not strict disciplinarians having been started by a French lady with a strong family background. Our education was much broader with far less specialising. The big advantage of boarding was the time we had for hobbies and crafts. Our class unit was very special even in our free time. When things went wrong, we missed our parents of course but there was always someone free to listen and advise. I think, with hindsight, that the family unit did suffer because we only saw our parents in the holidays and holiday times became very special times to be filled with all sorts of exciting activities. Our parents missed the day-to-day problems we had experienced and missed the exchange of news. However, I happily stayed to finish my education at boarding school.

On reflection, I realise that so much has changed since I was born seventy-plus years ago. Not the obvious scientific changes but the whole way of life. We lived through a war that greatly affected our way of life and have progressed through discoveries and inventions to a life made much easier by machines. However, so much has been lost in terms of values and social responsibilities that I wonder if this generation will look back in seventy-plus years and feel there has been progress or that they have lost too much?

Alice Street, Tidal Basin, E16

By Patricia Butcher

10 Alice Street, Tidal Basin, London E16 – this was the first address that Patricia Rosina or 'Pat' (as she was known as) had to memorize. "Just in case you get lost" warned her mother. Pat was born in the early thirties in an old council terrace house, probably built in the 1800s when the Victoria Docks were being built. Alice Street itself was a narrow cobbled street, gas-lit by hand by a special lamp-lighter and from No 10 to the left were three little shops - then an off-licence and a tavern which ran to the corner of Victoria Dock Road. Across the road were the actual Victoria Docks. To the right of No 10 were five more terraced houses and then a little vegetable shop which ended the block. Further up Alice Street was St Luke's Church and Infant School and the street eventually led to Rathbone Street where the well-known east-end Rathbone Street Market was held.

Patricia Rosina lived at No 10 with her mother and father and two younger sisters. Previously, her maternal grandparents had lived there and reared a family of six children and her grandfather still had a room where he stayed when he was home from sea. The family all slept in the front bedroom that looked out onto the street, the third bedroom (known as the "off-room") was not used as it was supposed to be haunted. It was never opened but who, or what, haunted it no-one really knew. The house itself was three-up and two-down with a scullery and a cold water copper for washing. There was an outside toilet with a shortened door that Pat thought was a good thing because she could look under it to see if there were any feet on show before she charged in. When the toilet paper ran out, Pat would help to 'string' the cut paper, newspaper mainly, to help her mother. The back-yard had not a blade of grass growing but the sisters could make some lovely mud pies at times. The two rooms downstairs consisted of a front room and a kitchen. The sisters were not allowed in the front room as this was a special room for visitors. There were armchairs, a settee, a huge aspidistra in a lovely coloured bowl on a special table, a fireplace with an embroidered screen and a mantle-piece with all kinds of coloured glass vases and bowls. Across the fireplace wall were three pictures which Pat would stand and look at and never get bored - one was a picture of a little boy standing on a stool being questioned by some sort of military 'committee' entitled `Where is your Father?` and the second picture was of a stag with huge antlers standing at bay on a hillside sniffing the air - this was called `The Monarch of the Glen`. This picture was above the fireplace. The third picture was known as either `The Blue Boy` or `Bubbles` - it was a cute little boy with fair curly hair dressed in blue, blowing bubbles on a pipe – he was very pretty. It was a special treat for the sisters to go into the room and just look.

Another favourite past-time for Pat and her sisters was to sit in the passage with the front door open and watch the people go by. It was always a busy street as it was so near the docks where people worked and seamen, in all kinds of national dress, would walk. The street was the local children's playground - a place where they had fun. Pat attended St. Luke's School and found school life easy as she was taught to read by her father and grandfather, who bought many books for the girls, and the local kids accepted her as their leader. Pat's best friend was the little boy who lived in the greengrocer's at the end of the terrace. It had a wooden floor which was always very dusty with large bags of vegetables standing around. This little boy had more toys than anyone else in the street - mainly tin toys, all bright colours, that you would wind with a key and then run over the dusty floor amongst the customers' feet. Pat felt very proud to be his friend.

When the gang of local children got together, they used to roam up the street towards the Vic Dock Road, passing the shops and looking in to see if there were any offers of 'goodies'. The 'lady' next door in the first shop, a sweet shop, would give them any sun-dried chocolate or damaged sweets. The next shop, where they sold saveloys and pease pudding and also faggots, was known as The Dairy but the children didn't get much from there. This shop did, however, have a lovely sawdust floor upon which you could draw patterns with your feet. The next shop was a little grocer's and in those days biscuits were packed in tin boxes and there were many broken ones and, if children were good, they would get a handful or so. Then came the off-licence which was not very interesting to children and stood next to the 'beer-shop' as it was called – real name 'The Tavern'. The children liked to look inside The Tavern because of the lights, the shiny brass, sometimes music and always a warm smell. The beer was delivered weekly in great wooden barrels and this was an event for the kids. The barrels were carried on a cart, or a 'dray' as it was called, which was drawn by gigantic horses and very big men who unloaded the barrels and dropped them by ropes down a special ladder to the beer-shop`s cellars. The horses were fed with nosebags while they were being unloaded and Pat always watched them carefully in case they were being suffocated. At times, the horses would pee and the kids would squeal with wonder at the amount of pee that came from the horse. It was a real sight.

Around the corner, on the Vic Dock Road, was a pawn-shop whose window was always filled with interesting bits and pieces to be looked at and commented on. But, for children, a walkway bridge across the road was one of the best places. This bridge ran over the dock`s railway lines and steam trains were always chuffing along and passing under the bridge. The children would play at losing their way in the fog of steam and the steam and smoke would blow up the girls' skirts and the boys' trouser legs which was all very funny to them.

The young lives of these little east-enders were happy ones although they suffered from various illnesses at times as it was not a healthy area. Seamen from around the world docked with more than just their cargo but the sisters' mother loved them and looked after them well. These tales are just a few of the many that could be told but all changed when a thing called an air-raid shelter was put in the sisters' backyard. Another story that I hope I can tell another time.

A Continental Holiday

By Dorene Carr

I was seven years old when I first went 'on the Continent' and, as this was 1949 and most of my friends did not have any kind of holiday, rather unusual. I was born in August 1941 and my brother 16 months later. Our sister did not arrive until 1953 so she has no part in these memories.

From mid 1943, my father - a tall dark and handsome man (a bit of a cliché, I know, but true for all that) had spent his time in the army fighting his way through firstly North Africa and then Italy via Sicily. We were at my grandmother's when he returned in 1946 and, finding the house empty, was told by a neighbour that we were at Win's mother's house. I remember the knock on the door and my grandmother telling Win (my mother) that it was someone for her. Next thing we knew, my mother was being swung around by a stranger who we were told was "your father". Even the word meant little to us; he had been talked about but as all our relatives and friends had fathers who were away fighting, the word "father" was a very unknown quantity. Both my brother and I soon realized that our life of running wild was over and that our father had the wanderlust in him.

Army surplus stores provided a tent and accessories and soon we were off most weekends on my father's motorbike with a sidecar that was hardly roomy for the equipment never mind my brother and me. The bike itself had been parked in the kitchen throughout the war and every week my mother would kick start it, rev it for a while, and then stop it until next time.

We had some great weekends - in fact they became ordinary to us. Our father would stand at the back door, look out at the weather and say "Okay Winnie! We're off in half an hour"and my mother would drop everything and load up the sidecar. Where my father was concerned, his word was law and she would have followed him to the moon if that was his destination. His destination in 1948 was the Europe he had recently returned from and that is where the two of them went on the solo motorbike.

They were away for three weeks and, during that time, my brother and I were billeted with Auntie Joan (mother's sister) and her children Anne - three months my senior -and John who was about my brother's age. We spent the time causing the sort of havoc that five and six-year-olds seem naturally to do while Auntie Joan smiled at us and let us get on with it. In all, she had eleven children and, at seventy, very few wrinkles. The 'letting them get on with it' policy obviously worked.

The following year, all four of us crossed a still very ruined France to Switzerland for a holiday that remains in the memory despite all those I have had since. The motorbike was the same one my parents had used in 1948, but with a bigger sidecar attached. I have no recollection of the make of bike or sidecar but it was the usual sidecar design with a small dickey seat inside a pull down flap at the back. My mother and I took it in turn to ride pillion, something I was quite used to doing as I had gone out with my father on the solo many times. At our age, distance was impossible to imagine. We were told that we were going a long way; over the sea and over mountains. We were aware of hills, having been brought up on the foothills of the Pennines, but mountains were still only pictures in books.

Our journey took us down the Great North Road and eventually to Dover where we spent the night, ready for the first ferry next morning. We stayed in a guesthouse, that in itself being an adventure as we had only ever camped until then. My brother and I were given a very tiny attic room with the only light coming from a small window in the roof. However, because it was July, darkness did not come too soon. Next morning, we awoke at the crack of dawn to the scream of seagulls around the docks and the smell of salt in the air. We sailed on the ferry Lord Warden and the bike and sidecar were put into a net and lifted on to the boat and down into the hold. Everyone seemed to be aiming to be the last in the queue for the boat, as the last on was the first off. I can't remember now how long the journey lasted. We were lucky that the sea was calm because we had a meal on the boat so as not to waste time on arrival in France and I found out the following year that I was not a very good sea traveller. My father wanted to be on the road to Paris as soon as we landed.

As we approached Calais, we saw the ruins of a house - two end walls and nothing but rubble in the middle - standing stark against the sky. That was the beginning of our journey through France.

Something I still remember is the smell of France that first day; it was a warm and spicy smell that got into your nose and, I realized years later, came from the garlic and herbs used by the French in cooking - to me at the time, very exotic. The next surprise was driving on the 'wrong' side of the road - a bit unnerving at first but we soon regarded this as normal and there wasn't much in the way of traffic on any of the roads we used. Toilet facilities were crude to say the least; we had an ordinary lavatory in our house so to be shown into a room with a hole in the tiled floor and two handles waist high to hang on to caused much hilarity between my brother and I when we compared notes later. I think we were both a bit scared of falling down the hole at first but this too was soon normal. How very accepting children are.

We reached Amiens that day and, as it was late, found rooms above a bar in a building shaped like a wedge - narrow at the front where the door was and then widening as it went back. I don't remember much else about Amiens. It was late when we got there and we were away early next morning on the road to Paris. It became our habit to picnic at lunchtime and, to that end, we always stopped in the last village before our meal to buy fresh French bread. We bought milk, tomatoes and melons from farm gates and always seemed to have plenty of cheese. As soon as we stopped, my brother and I had to find water for our mother's tea. Travelling the way we did meant there was no room for unnecessary items but tea was necessary to ensure our mother's holiday enjoyment. So, whilst we looked for water, my father lit the primus stove. That was the routine through the following years too.

A Continental Holiday

Our destination on 'Day Two' was Paris although we stayed outside the city at a camping ground in Fontainebleu forest. Not many people camped there in 1949 but the camp became busier in later years. I think we spent two nights at Fontainebleu. I know that, the next day, we visited the city taking the lift up the Arc de Triomphe. From the top it seemed you could see the whole world. I loved it but my brother, who did not like heights, was very unhappy so we did not visit the Eiffel Tower but went to Montmartre to watch the artists and Notre Dame where my mother and I were forbidden entry because we had bare arms. We had the required headscarves but no cardigans. C'est la vie! Later we walked down the Champs Elyssee and drank something at a pavement cafe; another surprise, the French were eating in the street!

Some areas of England were badly bombed during the war, causing terrible damage to places like London and Coventry, but on the whole the villages were thankfully untouched. In some areas of France, the armies fought for every street and sometimes every building which left lots of small villages flattened to just rubble. We stopped for lunch outside one such village and my brother wandered off only to return carrying an unexploded shell. His "look what I found, Dad" caused a bit of a flutter from my mother but my father soon put things to rights. Now we understood why he had been telling us not to touch certain "things".

The following few days saw us travel through rural France to the most frightening part of the journey - crossing the Jura mountains. Every now and then we would stop on one of the hairpins and watch others making their way up to the top of the pass. With hindsight, I suppose we stopped to prevent the bike from over-heating. In 1949 there was little in the way of safety barriers across the mountains - in fact, there was nothing to stop you going over the edge if you got too close. It was alright until you met something coming the other way, then it got really scary. I remember sitting in the dickey seat for miles with my eyes closed.

Our final destination was always Switzerland but exactly where in Switzerland was never decided in advance – all we ever agreed was that it would need to be within easy driving distance of Geneva. So, this year, we camped on the lake half way between Geneva and Lausanne on a site with showers (cold water only) which we had never experienced before. Our tent was pitched very close to the water, among lots of others - mostly Swiss families - and it was not long before my brother and I made friends and were even able to utter a few foreign words. My parents made friends with a young couple called John and Alice (they were doctors, I think) and the following year they took us to watch the Swiss Grand Prix from the flat roof of an apartment block along the route. Access to the roof was from a balcony reached through a sash window above a bed that was being slept in. The occupant did not even wake up as we all scrambled over him.

I remember little of 1949 in Geneva apart from enjoying an ice-cream by the fountain. Most of my memories are of the lake, the tent and the rubber dinghy my father inflated for us to go fishing. I caught my first and last fish there - I was so horrified by it struggling on the hook that I dropped the lot overboard. Fishing was not for me. I recently asked my brother what he remembered of that holiday and he surprised me by saying, "Oh, the wasp nest on the end of the jetty". I have no memory of that at all. He described the jetty and I could picture it but no wasp nest, nothing like that. Our memories are very similar in most other respects but, when I think of it, his are almost all of things which would have interested boys whilst mine are general impressions.

Before our holiday my mother had knitted a swimsuit for me in red and white wool which I wore most of each day. She had to make running repairs the first time I wore it into the water as the colour ran and it stretched almost to my knees. I burn very easily so my skin was red and flaking to match the swimsuit more often than not, or covered with calamine lotion - no one had thought of sun block at that time!

Our holiday lasted twenty-one days from start to finish; five days to get there, five to get back and eleven in the middle. The weather was wonderful for most of the time although we did have one very frightening thunderstorm crossing the Jura on the return journey. Our route back to Calais was almost the same as the one out with just a few changes to visit specific places, arriving in Calais in time for the last boat of the day. Back in England, my father rode the bike through the night up the Great North Road whilst we children slept in the sidecar and our mother rode pillion.

At school in September we were all asked about our holidays and, on a big map, I was told to point out where we had gone. Most of the children in my class did not believe that we had crossed the sea, especially as most of them had never even seen the sea. It had been an exciting and sometimes scary experience but not particularly special as my father was always taking us somewhere at weekends - Blackpool, the Lake District, Scarborough etc. as well as holidays in Cornwall or Devon. I did not appreciate that my life was different in that, apart from one other family who had a car, all the rest of our neighbours had no form of family transport apart from bicycles so no holidays away. To us, packing things up and going off on the bike was normal living and, in 1949, we had just gone a bit further than usual.

Marni

By Meg Hinds

I was born in Adolphus Street, Seaham, County Durham. We lived in a small flat above a shop called Mosey Bells in accommodation called Tenement Buildings. (In later years this street was demolished and rebuilt with modern houses and renamed Shakespear Street.)

The flat had no running water so we had to fetch it up in buckets from the downstairs yard and carry it back upstairs for the day's use. My older sister and I had to do our share of collecting the water.

The shop below us was owned by a very gentle kind man. He used to let my sister and I bring our toy dustpans and brushes and sweep up for him and, in return, he gave us pennies or sweets. We sometimes saved our pennies to buy Mam birthday or Christmas presents.

A girl who lived a few yards away from us became my good friend and we had some great adventures. Jennifer and I got up to mischief most of the time but one event will stick in my memory for all time. We were allowed to go anywhere we liked knowing we would be safe but, that said, we were always told never to go to a local place called The Green Drive. We were never told why and we never asked - we just obeyed. However, being bored one day we decided to go and find out what it was like. We had a great time. Our mothers always knew that, come what may, we would always be home for dinner. Children seem to have a built-in body clock to tell them when dinner time was so we did not need watches. This next part was told to me in later years by my Mam. When we did not return at the proper time, my parents became worried and called the police. When asked if they had any idea of where we would go they said anywhere except The Green Drive so, of course, that was the first place they looked and - yes - that's where we were. I remember being brought home sitting on the back seat of the police car, very dirty.

We were greeted by a street full of anxious people - in particular - two very relieved mums, pleased to see us safe. We were given a great big hug although it was a toss up between that or a good belting. When we went indoors I was given a hot bath and dinner and bed. As I said before, to get a bath the water had to be brought up and heated on the stove then poured in to the tin bath in front of the fire. It was not like today where you just turn the taps and water flows out. We had no inside toilet so it meant going down to the backyard to the toilet which we shared with our neighbours.

Living so close to the sea, we children used to go down nearly every day to the beach. It was where I learned to swim. I was pushed in, so I had to learn in a hurry but this did not put me off as I have enjoyed swimming all my life. While at the beach, we would go winkle-picking. For those that do not know, winkles are a type of water snail. We would then bring them home and mum would boil them till cooked and we would pull out the meat with a pin and eat them. They were very salty but I enjoyed them. We ate a lot of seafood as it was so easy to buy it straight off the fishing boats or, sometimes, the fishermen brought their catches up to the cliff top to sell.

Sometimes, our Dad took my sister Pat and I with him to buy seafood and when we got near we had to cross a small railway line which carried the coal in trucks from the mine our dad worked at. If any trucks were due the guard would wave his red flag and we would have to wait for them to pass before the guard would let us go over. When it was dark the guard would swing his lantern to warn people. After Dad had bought the crabs etc. we would go home and he would cook them. Mam and Dad would eat the body meat and us kids would be given all the legs. We picked out the meat with hair-grips - it was lovely.

In 1953, our brother Robert was born. They said he was so small he could fit into a pint pot although he made up for it in later life. In June of the same year it was the Queen's coronation. Mam dressed Pat and I in identical outfits and we did look marvellous. The night before Mam put our hair into pipe cleaners to curl it [no modern rollers back then] and it was painful come the morning when she took them out. Anyone who has had this done will know what I mean. She would then brush our hair out using a metal type brush and she had a heavy hand, bless her. Ouch. When we were ready, we joined everyone else in the street having a great time and waving our Union Jacks. When all the excitement had died down, our cousin Jean asked Mam if she could take us girls for a walk so off we went. Part of the walk took us to the docks area so we stood at the railing to watch the boats come in. I was swinging my foot and, to my horror, my brand new shoe flew off. We looked around for help and there was a man fishing near us. He tried to hook the shoe but it was not to be and so with help I limped home. Was I in trouble! It was my first and last pair of slip-on shoes. I was never allowed to forget the incident and people thought it extremely funny - the story did the rounds for many years.

It soon became time for me to start at Viceroy Street School, just up from where we lived. I was not there very long as we moved to Wynyard Street [the "Wide Back" as it was locally known - no idea why but presumably because it was a very wide road] in Dawdon and I went to Dawdon Infants. Later, we moved across the playground to the girls' junior school. It was in the infants school that I met Liz who became my very best friend and, very quickly, we were inseparable. We did get up to lots of mischief - in particular, we often went to her home for lunch and, as she lived above her parents' butcher shop in a flat, we would sit at the open window eating our sandwiches and dropping pieces down on to ladies' hats. The game was to see how many hats we could hit and Liz always won as she had a better aim than me. I often wonder what the ladies thought when they took off their hats. At the time, we thought it funny but, as I write this now, I am cringing.

Sometime later, we moved into a colliery house a few streets away. When we moved in, the house did not have a bathroom so we still had to use the tin bath, again in front of the fire. Although we did have running water, we still had to go to the bottom of the yard to the outside toilet and it was cold - freezing in winter! I was nine years old before we got a bathroom fitted. In a way, I missed the old bath times but I am sure my Mam did not! Until I had children of my own I never fully realised just how much hard work it must have been. It was around this time that we also got our first television set and I remember Pat and I being very excited. We were jumping up and down, telling the man to hurry up and fit it quickly as it was a Monday and Bobby Thompson was on [a great northern comedian].

I'm not sure what age I was when it started but I went through some years of just eating bread and jam for every meal. I must have driven my poor Mam mad with it! She even took me to the doctors but all he said was not to worry and I would eat properly when I was ready. I know she was very embarrassed when we had visitors because there we were, me with my plate of sandwiches and the rest with roast dinners etc. It must have looked as though that was all they would let me have. I have more than made up for it in later life!

The street we lived on was quite steeply sloped so when we played our ball games it could be a nightmare if you were the one catching and missed. It was a long run down and back up. We played many games, a lot of which we invented ourselves. We had our favourites of course, like Top and Whip. One game we called 'Knocky Nine Doors' and this involved knocking on peoples' doors and running away. These games were never meant maliciously - we were just having fun. When we started to get pocket money, we got threepence a day and sixpence on a Saturday [pre-decimal money]. Monday to Friday, I would go down to Lord Street and buy a pennyworth of bruised fruit then up to our local shop to get a pennyworth of sherbet, a half penny stick of liquorice and a half pennyworth of Blackjacks. On Saturdays, we went to the matinees at the cinema. Our sixpence covered our entry fee and popcorn.

We saw our heroes like Zorro, Roy Rogers etc and, when we came out, we would pretend we were them all the way home. During these years, apart from the normal childhood ailments, there was a two week period when I developed a strange illness. I had these raised purple flat lump-like blotches on my legs and I could not walk. The doctor came every day and I had quite a lot of visitors; everyone was worried, even Mr.Williamson the local shop-keeper. He told my Mam to come to his flat door when his shop was closed if ever I needed or wanted anything that Mam did not have in; he said it did not matter if it was day or night and was so very kind. I don't know if Mam was ever told what the illness was but I was never told.

Life went on pretty much the same and then it was time for the Eleven Plus exams. I knew I could pass them but I did not want to go to the grammar school - I wanted to go with my friends to Camdon Square Secondary. I have since regretted that decision but hindsight is a wonderful thing. My teachers knew why I had done it and were not best pleased with me but there was nothing they could do. So after the summer holidays, off I went to Camdon School and for the most part I enjoyed it. Just down from the school, on the corner, there was a baker's shop and we went every lunchtime to buy a penny loaf freshly made. They were about three inches square and tasted delicious. I liked most of the games and sports at school - particularly netball and hockey. One day, playing hockey, I did not know Liz was behind me and swung my stick and hit her in the face. It was awful - she bled quite a lot and it was a wonder she hadn't lost any teeth. I felt terrible about this for a long time although she did forgive me because it had been an accident.

There was a lovely park in Dawdon and we often walked in. At Easter time, and when we were younger, we would take our 'paste eggs' [hard boiled and hand-decorated] to roll down the slope until the shell cracked which meant we could eat the egg inside. But, by the time we had been at Camdon School for a couple of years, we were into our teens and all the latest fashions like the 'cha cha', mini skirts, special make-up and hair styles and, of course, the pop music of the time. My two most favourite bands were The Beatles and The Rolling Stones. Like all their fans, we had our hair styled like The Beatles and had to wear 'Chelsea Boots'. We thought we looked the business.

When I was fourteen, my sister Pauline was born. I was like a mother hen and, when home, liked nothing better than to look after her and take her out in her pram. She seemed like my baby sometimes. Because she could not talk until she was four years old and could not pronounce my name, I soon became known as 'Marnie' [hence the title of this story].

Pauline was born in the March of the same year I left school. In those days we left at fifteen but, as my birthday was in the summer holiday, I was actually only fourteen when I left. Sadly, my friend Liz and I got different jobs and slowly drifted apart as other things and people came into our lives - a real shame but these things happen. Of course, throughout these years, boyfriends came and went. My first job was at Woolworths in Church Street in Seaham and I worked there for three years. Some months after starting work, I met a man who would become my husband but that, as they say, is another story...

An Autobiographical Sketch

By Derek Maldon Fitch

I was born at Hazeleigh Grange on 21st April 1922, the second son of Maldon and Ethel Fitch.

Like Admiral Nelson, whose mother died at the age of forty-two when he was only nine and left a lasting impression on him, so likewise I had the same experience except that it was my father who died aged forty-two when I was nine. He and his younger brother were killed by Germans in April 1931 at Mundon.

My father and his regiment, the 20th Middlesex, had had mustard gas set against them at the Battle of Loos in 1916. Invalided from the army in 1917, it was a choice between an outdoor occupation or the rest of his life in a sanatorium since the gas had affected his lungs so he went into farming. He survived somewhat longer than his other younger brother, Leonard, who served with the Essex Yeomanry and suffered a mustard gas attack during the Battle of Ypres. After a short spell in Colchester Hospital, Leonard went to stay with my parents who were then living at Limbourne Park, Mundon, but he had only been with them a few days when he suffered a massive haemorrhage and died in my mother's arms. He was only 22 - a tragedy since he had just passed his final exams to become a surveyor and had just become engaged to a Colchester girl.

My mother was widowed at thirty-nine and granted a Widow's Pension which, in those days, was an insulting pittance. Education of the first child, my sister, was taken care of by the Ministry of Pensions. Any other children were not allowed for. Fortunately, my father had been a Freemason and so I was sent to their school for war orphans – a boarding school at Wanstead. My introduction to this monastic establishment was not a pleasant one since the junior house master used to physically abuse the boys. But then it happened that, one half-term when our mothers were allowed to visit us, I was sporting a black eye which I had been given by this master. My mother wanted to know how it had happened and, ultimately, I and another boy who had been maltreated and his mother appeared before the school governors; the master in question was dismissed at the end of term.

The remainder of the staff were good as was my education but only to a point; at the age of sixteen, irrespective of what stage you had reached in your education, the guillotine was dropped; in other words, we had an unsatisfactory truncated education. Further education and universities were never mentioned, although the headmaster/chaplain of the school was an M.A. (Oxon). Careers were never mentioned. My sister and I would have fared better if we had been left at the Maldon Grammar School which we had attended briefly between 1931-2. This underlines the deplorable state of education back in the thirties. I attended Wanstead for six years between 1932-8

which was the sum total of my education. The Royal
Wanstead School is no longer – the judiciary have taken
over and it is now Snaresbrook Crown Court.

Now the war years...At age seventeen in 1939, I joined
the R.A.F. attending a wireless operator's course at
Cranwell. From there, I went to the seaplane base at
Felixstowe where I remained until 1942 when I was sent to
India and Burma for four years. We joined a convoy which
formed up at Clydebank off Greenock and in March 1942
set sail for India. It was a large convoy, under naval escort,
to India via Freetown and Cape Town where we stopped off
for three or four days. Many of us were entertained in the
homes of South Africans and we climbed part of the way up
Table Mountain and visited the Kirschenbosch Botanical
Gardens.

After landing at Bombay, we went to Victoria Station
and boarded a troop train. Then followed a very long
journey across India to Calcutta via Lucknow. From
Calcutta, we went on to Cuttack on the Mahandi Delta in
Orissa State where we were to serve with No. 353 Squadron
– a Dakota squadron whose role it was to drop supplies to
the 14th Army in Burma. My particular unit had the role of
defending the squadron against ground and air attack, not
that the Japanese had very much air power in the Indo-
Burma theatre. In 1943, our unit was sent to Secunderabad
in the Hyderabad State in the south of India. Here we were
trained as commando units. We became the founding fathers
of what is nowadays the RAF Regiment with their base at
Honiton in Suffolk and who now have a paratroop as well
as a commando role. We were trained in jungle warfare,

unarmed combat, assault courses carried out under live fire, and trained to use machine guns and hand grenades. We were kitted out in jungle green khaki drill and Australian bush hats (which are the answer against the tropical sun and monsoon rains) and in this outfit you merge completely with the jungle.

After the unit's rest at Otercamand Hill station up in the Nilgiri Hills we were all transported by troop train up the east coast of India to the north-east frontier - what is now known as Bangladesh. We were then ferried across the river Brahmaputra with all our equipment.

Our role in Burma was to defend forward air-strips and carry out reconnaissance patrols, firstly in the Arakan coastal strip in 1943. My unit was to be involved in the siege of Imphal and the Battle of Kohima which marked the turning point when the Japanese were driven back through Burma.

In 1944/5, I joined another unit and, with them, was to go right through Burma terminating at Rangoon and the battle of Meiktula where the Japs made their last stand on the airfield before being driven across the River Salween into Siam. My unit were engaged in this action and several of my colleagues were killed - including the C.O. and his runner who were both shot through the head by a Jap sniper from up in a palm tree. The sniper was then shot by one of our marksmen gunners. Our casualties rest in the Rangoon War Cemetery.

We ended up encamped in the jungle at Prome on the banks of the River Irrawaddy where I contracted my last attack of dysentery and was flown back to the military field hospital in Dacca and from there via Calcutta to Darjeiling for a month's convalescence at 7,000 ft up in the Himalayan foothills. Quite a joy after Burma with its tropical heat averaging 120F, monsoon rains, flash floods, swamps with their leeches, the jungle with its snakes and all this while having to sleep on the floor with just a groundsheet to protect against the damp. When my spinal trouble started showing itself about ten years ago, I immediately thought of those days and consider them to be a contributory factor.

My occupational pension is a police one. I belonged to a special detachment of armed Police Officers responsible for the security of MI5 but retired from the force in 1977 on compassionate grounds; my mother had become a chronic invalid and died in 1978.

I married the widow of Rev. Alan Carey - Muriel (Pixy) - a Kings Lynn girl. Alan, as a major with the Royal West Kents, had also been at Kohima where my unit had been although we did not know that at the time.) Muriel and I were married in Cheam village in Surrey by my cousin Canon John Fitch and my other cousin Admiral Sir Richard Fitch who was the 2nd Sea Lord and my Best Man. Richard has since died and Muriel died at Christmas 1999 having become a chronic invalid.

As a result of an augmentation of honour signed by the Queen, the College of Arms granted to me under Letters Patent, signed and sealed by the King of Alms, a badge and battle standard in recognition of my services in Burma. The badge consists of the Burmese mountain partridge and the

Burmese orchid named after, and in honour of, Lt. General Albert Fytche who was a Governor of Burma in the 18th century.

My battle standard, published in a previous Penny Farthing, consists of the badge and my arms with my motto "facta non verba" (deeds not words).

Social Work Stories

– an excerpt By Charles Middleton

Many people I've met over the years, including friends and relatives, have said that they could write a book about all the things that have happened to them in both their lives and their careers. These people have ranged from pilots to market traders and are made up of individuals from all walks of life who have a variety of anecdotal stories to tell. Some of the happenings have come from time spent in military service or in employment whilst others recall events in their lives or stories about places where they have lived and people they have met. I've learned that very few people actually write down these important personal memories but their stories relate to periods of social history that will be of great interest and importance to future generations and will be lost forever if they are not handed down in written form rather than 'word of mouth'. With 'word of mouth', stories tend to get changed and distorted over periods of time. The written form also has the advantage of presenting all of us with the opportunity to leave a part of ourselves and our lives behind so that we will not be forgotten by the coming generations.

My own story starts in 1971 when, after twenty-six years working as an 'engine man' on the railway at Stratford in the East End of London, I decided to change careers – to move into Social Work. As part of this process, I needed to acquire some typing skills and, with two months to go before I left my job as an engine driver, I decided to write about my years on the railway. I knew this would help me to acquire the typing skill I would soon need.

When I eventually retired from Social Work at the end of 1994, I found my poorly- typed, grammatically erroneous and mis-spelled narrative at the bottom of an old cupboard and, with encouragement from my son (a long-time railway enthusiast), re-typed it on to my newly acquired computer. When friends read through the draft, they thought I should try and get the manuscript published and 'Stratford, A Locoman Remembers' was published in 2000.

I therefore blame my son for this second narrative (which relates to my 'early days' as a Social Worker) since I found the first experience of writing so pleasurable and now have a taste for it.

Social Work: The Early Days

Social work is one of the least understood professions and can be testing. For example, Social Workers often receive a lot of criticism when someone is removed from a difficult situation (be it a child or an adult) but can also be criticised for not removing someone. My hope for this excerpt, therefore, is that it will help to provide readers with a greater understanding of Social Work – its complexity, its range and the real expectations of social workers. I also hope that I can provide a glance of what really lies behind the public façade of the Social Services.

Following my resignation from 'British Railways', I took up my new career at the National Society for the Prevention of Cruelty to Children's 'School of Social Work' which was housed in their main office next door to Broadcasting House in the heart of London's West End. Here I joined a group of eighteen trainee Inspectors for an eighteen month course that was intended to prepare us for our new jobs. We all came from a diverse range of previous occupations that included a milkman, a policewoman, a nanny, a factory manager, a pop guitarist and, of course, an engine driver. Each of us brought with us a variety of life experience that we were able to use to enrich our training for our future careers.

The course itself came as a culture shock to most of us and some of us fell by the wayside, failing to complete the rigorous training regime. The problem was not usually one of poor academic achievement but related more to the realisation that we would need to look deeply into our own emotional baggage in order to gain an insight into the lives of those people with whom we would be working with and assisting. If we could not sort our own lives out, how could we be expected to help other people?

The course - consisting of a series of lectures that covered sociology, physiology, psychology, law and child development - lasted for eighteen months and provided the basis for our future work. The course also included work placements in many other agencies. It was hard work but well-structured and helped to prepare us for the tasks we were soon to face.

We also spent some of the time in one of the NSPCC's Group offices that were near to London under the supervision of a 'Field Work Tutor'. This was the time when we came face to face with clients and quickly learnt the interviewing techniques and investigation skills that were an essential part of a range of knowledge we required in our new roles. We also had to learn a very hard lesson; that believable, nice people could inflict both physical and psychological injuries on their own children and that children who were being abused would lie to protect their parents. We also heard anecdotal stories told by older Inspectors which may have contained degrees of exaggeration. Most of these Inspectors had only recently come out of the regulation uniform although some of the 'old timers' persisted in wearing the suit provided but not the cap. Many were reluctant to give up their uniform as they felt it had given them some authority in the past and that it was respected by the general public. They also found it very useful for getting into houses because most people did not like their neighbours to see the Inspector hammering on their door for any length of time and would let them into the house before the news spread through the neighbourhood.

These old inspectors also taught us many of the 'tricks of the trade' that were frowned upon by our lecturers and would not have any place in today's social work ethos. Here are examples of some of them. One inspector told me that, in days past, if young children were left alone in the house then the best way to gain entry was to hammer on the doors and windows until the children cried. It was then a simple matter to get the police to break in, without a warrant, as there were children in the house "in some obvious distress".

Another Inspector told me that, in his younger days, he had gone to visit a lady with an Inspector whose roots were still entrenched in the days of the 1930s. The lady had been complaining that her husband had gone off her and no longer cared for her. To her husband's surprise, the old Inspector said he thought her husband was a sensible man and said he couldn't see why anyone would want to touch her - even with a 'barge-pole'. He said she was an absolute disgrace. He suggested that she took a good look at herself in the mirror as he failed to see how she had ever allowed herself to get in such a state. The young Inspector was shocked at this and felt very upset for the lady concerned. However, to his surprise, when they next visited the lady and her husband the situation had improved. The woman was clean, tidy, well-groomed and looked very attractive. The husband had found his wife to be the object of his affection once again and the marriage was on the mend. Although this may be an extreme example, it does serve to remind us that the Social Worker does have to confront their client when it is appropriate and challenge their behaviour.

Another Inspector told me that when he had once visited the home of a single mother, he walked into the house after hearing a voice saying "Come in, I won't be a moment" only to find the client appear without any clothing on. He was not sure as to what to do, as he did not wish to upset her too much or spoil any professional relationship that may have existed between them. He stood his ground and said, "I'll come back when you are in a more sensible frame of mind, Rosie." This appeared to do the trick and he never had any further problems. I always felt that it was an answer I would have been proud of.

These stories formed an important part of our learning process and allowed us to benefit from others' wisdom and to learn from their mistakes.

The same Inspector also told me about another lady who would ring him up and ask if he could get her a pair of shoes. This appeared to be a strange request as she had a cupboard that was full of shoes. He soon realised that this lady had a very difficult and deprived childhood and had never been able to approach anyone for affection, nor could she cope if any form of kindness was shown towards her. He soon discovered that receiving shoes was, in a sense, a token of the fact that someone did care about her and this helped her towards making beneficial and appropriate relationships with other adults.

He also told me of a time when he was once offered a new suite of furniture by a local business who no longer required it. He knew just the family that were in dire need and made arrangements for it to be delivered to them the very next day. Imagine his surprise when he had six more self-referrals from the same street from individuals who claimed that they had family and child care problems and, by a strange coincidence, just happened to be in urgent need of three-piece suites.

This mixture of study and field practice allowed us to put what we had been taught into use in real life situations and we were often surprised by the results of our intervention.

Human behaviour is very predictable and when we found that our clients related to us in the same way that we had been taught that they would, we began to think that they had either read the same text books or that they were 'plants' - people recruited to test our newly acquired skills.

We were also taught that, when we challenged people on suspicion of abuse towards their children, many would be almost pleased to have been found out and would not be violent or angry towards us. We soon discovered that most of these parents knew that what they were doing to their children was wrong and, at long last, someone had come along who was going to challenge their behaviour and help them to overcome poor parenting at a level not even acceptable to them. They did not have the self-ability or means to change their own behaviour and here was an opportunity that they could not afford to miss.

Being new to the job, one of my expectations was that the people I would be visiting would be very angry and that I should expect a violent confrontation from big bullies. This proved to be far from the reality of the situation.

My very first home visit concerned a man who was the father of five children. He had suggested to his wife that she move in with her mother while he was working away from home. The wife and children moved in with her mother but, after she had not heard from her husband for a few days and had no idea of his whereabouts, she returned to their rented home only to find he had sold all their furniture and belongings. When she could not trace him, our assistance was requested and (with some help from a tip-off) the husband was traced to the area in which I was doing my first placement. So a home visit to this man became my first ever visit to a client on my own. "What sort of man could this be?" I thought. Who could do such a thing to his family? I was aware that he was working with a road building gang and I therefore had this vision of a great big violent navvy who would turn very nasty when I confronted him. I walked up the path to the house and took the door-knocker in my hand. I was shaking so much that my hand took on a life of its own and did the knocking for me! I was hoping that the door would not be opened and that I'd be able to go back to the office and say no-one was home but the door did open. However, the big surprise was that I was confronted, not by a big bully, but by a small timid ineffective looking man who was much more scared of me than I was of him. From my conversation with him, it appeared that he was an inadequate and anxious man and not the sort who'd be able to cope with looking after a wife and family. What he really needed was a mother figure who would take care of him.

I came away content with the promise that this man would send money to his wife and children on a regular basis although did make it clear that I'd heard he'd been a deserter from the army...As it turned out, this man did keep up the regular payments to his wife and children and I never had to mention the army again.

From this first home visit, I learned two things that would stay with me for the rest of my career in social work. The first was that I was being perceived as a person of great power and authority even though I had few options for action if individuals chose not to cooperate with me. People always believed that we had the power to enter their homes which we did not. We, of course, would always be as open and honest as we could be with our clients in order to gain their trust. The question we would ask once we had announced ourselves was "Can I come in?" The second lesson I came to learn was that most abusers suffered from inadequacies in their own childhood and life experience and needed compassion and help rather than punishment if they were ever to succeed as parents. They were always much more frightened of me than I was of them. Abusers also need those prepared to listen to them to have empathy and understanding.

I remember doing a project while on this course which involved me looking through the records held at Birmingham Central Library. Within the archives, the library had copies of all the local Societies' and NSPCC's Annual Reports going back to the 1880s. Looking through these, I found that they all included sample cases that could be used to help trace the development of social work over the years. Many of these cases highlighted the punitive responses of authorities towards clients in the early days of the Society progressing towards a far more humane, social work orientated and caring approach as the years went by.

In the early days, these Annual Reports showed how the Society took pride in the fact that children had been removed and parents given six months in prison "with hard labour". What on earth did this type of intervention do for any member of the family? The children removed then had to suffer the harshness of an institutional life and none of the family members would ever be able to return to any semblance of normality in their future lives.

Through these publications, I was able to trace a move towards present day ethical social work ideals - where the whole family is assisted to improve their own lives and their children's circumstances (rather than be punished) so that they can work towards desirable patterns of family dynamics and remain together as a family unit.

When my project partner and I presented our written findings, they were very favourably received and I know that we scored rather a lot of 'brownie points' for this piece of work.

Even today, some punitive measures remain in use (with the support of the legal system) despite the fact that they don't really assist either the children concerned or the family group. Once I had become a qualified Inspector, I had to deal with a case that (I was certain) involved incest within the family. In those days, society as a whole preferred to turn a blind eye to incest and would not accept that such incidents ever happened. The social worker raising cases relating to suspected incest was often portrayed as a troublemaker and frequently ended up being ridiculed by both the media and wider society. Incest never happened back then. Because of this, governing bodies preferred to keep a low profile in relation to incest with a non-committal attitude, always mindful of their dependence on public opinion. So, when I became suspicious of incest in this particular case, my best option was to go to the local police station. I suggested to the WP Sergeant that the local police should take over the inquiry in view of my suspicions - and in the light of what my informants would be prepared to tell them. Later that day, the police informed me that they had spoken to the informants and visited the relevant family with the result that the father had been arrested. He later confessed and the family were spared further suffering. Later, I received a Letter of Commendation from Head Office for the way I had dealt with this case. For my part, I felt that all I had done was to break up a family. If the law had not been so extreme, and allowed for family therapy instead, then a better solution could probably have been found (e.g. working closely with the father to address his problems).

The social work course was very thorough and effectively challenged our ability to do what could be seen as a stressful job. It played a critical part in preparing us well for the time when we would come to work alone in the field. If one looks at the Children's Act, you will see that there are three organisations that have the power to place a child before the (then) Juvenile Court and subsequently into care. These organisations are The Social Services Department, a Police Officer and an NSPCC Inspector. This meant that powers were granted to us as individuals and not to the organisation which employed us.

In our own areas we were powerful, although supervised and watched over by a Group Officer and Head Quarters staff. We were the general representatives of our appointed area and, as such, had responsibilities that ranged from selling houses (an early task) to liaising with and giving talks to volunteers, collecting cheques and being photographed doing so, as well as our duty to investigate child abuse cases as they occurred.

We were also expected to attend any royal engagements where children were present, such as the Children's Royal Variety Show and to help look after the children who were behind the scenes by managing doors, stairs and walkways. We also attended events where our President, the late Princess Margaret, was present. I always had a great deal of respect for her because she always took her role very seriously and we would often see her in the corridors of our Head Quarters in Riding House Street and would always receive a nice smile.

We also had to act as car park attendants when gardens were open to the public in aid of our charity. Although we had a lot of freedom to manage our own areas, it also gave us many additional duties and responsibilities. It was hard work but I gained a great deal of experience, personal satisfaction and fulfilment from my job.

Epilogue

I enjoyed the years that I spent in social work and feel the people I met gave me a great deal of satisfaction while sharing parts of their lives with me. It was a very rewarding experience which I will always carry with me. Times have changed within the area of social work, especially with regard to working with children. Much was based on mutual trust in my days but, of course, the system was always open to abuse. The stories I have told both respect and admire the people I have worked with and for. Life does have both its sad and humorous side and I hope that anyone who reads these stories will both laugh and share sorrow with the people involved - not laugh at or pity them.

What Did You Do In The War Grandad?

By Charles Middleton

My grandson recently asked me the question: "What did you do in the war granddad?" My ready answer was that I, like other boys of my own age, made a right nuisance of myself, got in the way and generally had a good time doing so.

Then I got to thinking. Had I done anything that had contributed to the war effort in the slightest way and, as was said at the time, "done my bit"? Maybe my efforts, in a very small way, had even prolonged the war? I decided that I would sit at my computer and look to see if I had done anything that was even a small contribution to the war effort.

When war broke out I was eight years old - getting on towards nine. We lived at the Stratford end of Leytonstone which is part of East London. Of course, I had many experiences of the Blitz and being bombed out but these memories will not necessarily form part of this narrative.

In the period of the so-called 'Phoney War', I was evacuated to Netswell in Essex and arrived at Burnt Mill Station which is now Harlow. Here is where I made my first contribution to the war effort. Nearby was a large sandpit and each morning I, with several of my school mates (we only had temporary use of schooling facilities in the WI centre), would arrive to start work. Our job was to fill up sandbags and, at the end of the morning, these were counted up by the foreman who would then pay us a penny for every three we had filled. This would give us at least sixpence and some of the bigger boys made a shilling or more. This was a great deal of money for a child in those days and was inappropriately mis-spent by all of us.

I was only away for about six weeks before returning home in time for the Blitz.

On returning to school at Downsell Road, a great deal of our time was spent in the air raid shelters. Boys and girls alike were all expected to be able to knit so that we could both contribute to the war effort and be kept busy in the shelters. We were all told to bring some wool and needles to school so that we could learn to knit and it was suggested that, if any of the girls were knitting something already, they could bring it.

I have always, even as a child, wanted to know how things worked and was always very investigative with my toys or in helping my father to make things - I could even mend shoes at a young age. My mother was always knitting for us; using the patterns from her magazine - the pink and blue 'Woman's Weekly'. My natural curiosity allowed me to learn skills such as crocheting and knitting and from an early age I could read knitting patterns, understand them and use four needles. I therefore asked my mother for some knitting to take to school and she gave me a sock she had started on four needles. When I sat in class knitting the teacher suddenly noticed me and said, "Come out that boy!" She asked me what I was doing and I said "Making socks, Miss". She appeared to be very surprised and asked me if I knew how to turn the heel. "Yes, Miss," I replied. It never occurred to me at the time that what I was doing was anything unusual but, thinking about it today, the story must have gone round the staff room. From then on I knitted several balaclava helmets in khaki for the troops. Later, I knitted soldier dolls for people - also from a pattern in 'Woman's Weekly' - dressed in the appropriate regimental uniform to suit the order. The dolls were usually for children whose fathers were away fighting although I did knit one ATS girl doll. I used to make sixpence profit on each one, which was a reasonable sum at the time.

I spent some time in both the Cubs and the Scouts but, although we were trained to work a stirrup pump to put out incendiary bombs and taught how to make a stretcher out of two jackets and two scout poles, I never really had a chance to use these skills as I was kept safely in the air raid shelters. We did however, as a group, go out sometimes to collect scrap metal for the war effort.

Although we boys generally made a nuisance of ourselves on recent bomb-sites, we were often gathered together to help the men who were making dangerous bombed buildings safe. They would put long ropes around the unsafe sections and a gang of us would form a team with the men on the rope and help pull the building down.

Another contribution to the war effort was to save our money and to buy sixpenny war savings stamps which were the forerunner of National Savings.

As I progressed to my senior school, us boys were set some tasks during our woodwork lessons. Apart from making toys, we built a huge slide for the Ellingham Road Day Nursery that cared for very young children while their mothers worked. My small role was to plane and sand the wooden treads that were to be made up into the steps. I am aware that the slide was still in use many years after the war and proudly pointed it out to whoever was driving past with me in my car.

Most people kept chickens and rabbits to supplement food rations. In order to help feed ours, I would go out on my bike with a friend to gather hay and anything else a rabbit would eat. We also gleaned for corn after the crop had been gathered to store as chicken feed.

One skill I learned was to kill chickens and to pluck them. On my first experience of this, my father killed the first one and then allowed me to kill the second one. This I did and was then in the shed with the chicken he had killed hanging on the door so that I could pluck it. Mine was lying on the bench beside me. All was quite and peaceful in the shed and I was absorbed in the task when, suddenly, the chicken I had 'killed' stood up and crowed. I had never been so scared in my life before and dashed into the house in panic and fright. At the time, I thought the chicken had come back to haunt me but it seemed I hadn't killed the chicken - I had merely stunned it. My father had to return and kill it properly.

With most of the men away, we boys often had to take on some of their tasks. This would include anything from banging a couple of nails in to helping to move furniture or some heavy lifting job. One lady, whose husband was away in the army, kept chickens and appeared at our door saying that a cat had attacked one of her young chicks that had only just started to grow feathers. As my father was at work, I was sent round to sort the matter out. The young bird had a long open wound on its side and the only option was to kill it to stop its suffering. I held the bird in between my legs, grasped its neck between my fingers, gave a sharp twist and pulled for all I was worth. To my surprise, I found myself with the body in one hand and the chicken's head in the other. The lady gave out a gasp of "Oh, my God!" and fainted. I knew what to do with a chicken but wasn't yet old enough to deal with a lady fainting at my feet.

My father kept two allotments near the railway at Temple Mills and I often spent time there, weeding and planting vegetables. This helped both our family and several neighbours and friends who benefited from the crops. I can still, to this day, recognise what type of vegetable is growing by just looking at the very first shoots. Working on the school allotment was another task I had to take part in but I have no idea where the crops went – perhaps they were produced so that the teachers and their families could eat better.

While on the subject of gardening I remember that, as motor vehicles were in short supply, nearly all the traders had horses and carts and so there was always a good supply of horse manure to be collected by us boys. We roamed the streets with our buckets and spades to collect manure and sometimes, if we were lucky, we could sell it. If not, it provided good manure for growing vegetables. I suppose we also gave a service by keeping the streets clean and hygienic.

With the shortage of fuel, my friend and I would queue up at a local factory that would let you take all the small off-cuts of wood at the end of the day – we used this wood as firewood at home.

As the war progressed, I got myself a paper round at a shop in Crownfield Road. My job was to deliver both morning and evening papers and to collect the money each week. In the evening I would have to go to Leyton Station to collect 'The Star, News and Standard' which were sold in quires. For those who don't know, a 'quire' was twenty-six newspapers.

I did have one or two adventures while delivering papers, including cycling along on my round when I suddenly found myself on a doorstep after an explosion. Today an ambulance would be called but, in those times, you just got back on your bike and carried on.

I always remember one particular morning which makes me realise how a child and an adult see situations so differently. There had been a land mine in Crownfield Road which had destroyed many of the houses on my round. One had only the door and the porch standing. I did not know what to do and I reasoned that if I did not deliver their paper they would arrive at the paper shop complaining, "That paper boy has not delivered my paper again!" I therefore pushed the paper through the letterbox of the standing door. Thinking about the incident today, I realise that the family were probably all dead and, even if they weren't, receiving their daily paper would have been the last thing on their minds.

During the later days of the war, I would go over to Eaton Manor Sports Ground with my friends to talk to the American soldiers that were camped there prior to D-Day. They would give us gum and sweets but, thinking about it afterwards, they appeared to have enjoyed talking to us and we may well have unknowingly helped with morale. When I talk about men being away and us boys fulfilling some of their roles, I think about playing darts for a team in the Leyton and Leytonstone District Firewatchers Darts League. I was just thirteen years old when I started to play because the men not away at war needed youngsters to make up a team. I don't know whether this helped to win the war - or whether it would look good on my 'CV' - but I enjoyed this time.

I suppose that, lastly, I must include my railway service. I started work at Stratford on the 10th April 1945 - just before the war ended. My job as a Junior Messenger was to work in the office collating the drivers' work sheets and going backwards and forwards to the main and other stations with letters and packages. I did have one of the wartime badges but lost it some years later when my hat (that the badge was attached to) blew off as we were approaching Clacton.

So this is a synopsis of what I did in the war. Did I do my 'bit' or could I have even prolonged the war? The reader must judge. What I do know is that the war ended too soon for me and for many boys like me. If it could have lasted until my fifteenth birthday, I would have been entitled to have a tin hat with M on it and cycled between the ARP posts with messages. Also, I didn't get to kill any Germans but, if the war had continued until I was an adult, I very much doubt I would still have wanted to.

Pictures
In My Mind

By Molly Middleton

When my ten-year-old granddaughter left a message on my answer phone the other day, I was somewhat confused. She wanted 'something from the 1930s' to take to school. She was not impressed when I suggested me! Well I am a product of the 1930s after all.

It turned out that my granddaughter was studying that period together with the Second World War years. I shouldn't have been surprised since my other six grandchildren had, in turn, made similar requests. I expect she will be reading 'Carrie's War' next.

Anyway, it started me thinking about that time in my life and how different it was from the life my granddaughter lives today. The later thirties and the early forties included the Second World War but also the years just before it. Being only a child back then, and not being concerned with the wider picture, my memories are more like snapshots from an album or pictures in a gallery for much of what went on. I accepted my life as 'ordinary' as children do, thinking all lives were exactly like mine. Of course, this is not so. Each life is unique, if similar to others' in some ways, but my experiences do illustrate the changes over time. So this is for my granddaughter.

Dear Elizabeth,

In re-visiting my childhood, I remember disconnected snatches and that's why I've likened it to a picture gallery with a selection of images, scenes and events. I was one month short of my fifth birthday when the war began and ten and a half when VE day happened, so the war covered my primary school years and my memories are coloured by a child's perspective. It is not the large events that I recall though - I remember lots of them, but then they were reported and shown on the newsreels at the pictures which is the reason my mother took me to every Saturday show from quite an early age. As I began to think about this piece of writing, I realised that my senses played a large part in recollecting the times so I have chosen to structure this around the smells, tastes, sounds, sights and feelings of my childhood.

For example, I am five again and my Daddy is getting me out of bed and carrying me along the passage. Then we go out into the garden and there is this lovely smell - a mixture of flowers and the night air and he takes me down some steps into a small place and lays me on a bunk. This place smelt of the earth - dank and musty. My mummy and daddy and the people from the upstairs flat are there and it gets noisy; bangs and whistles, and the boom of 'Big Bertha' - a large gun that was on the fields at the back of our road, and then I fall asleep. Later in the war, the little girl from upstairs and I slept in the cupboard under the stairs and the coal was moved outside. I cannot now ever go out into my garden on a summer night without noticing that same scent and I am back there again.

Pictures In My Mind

When I was little, there were not so many cars on our roads. The baker, the milkman, the coalman and other tradesmen would come round on carts pulled by horses while others like the greengrocer and the rag and bone man pushed hand carts. Each one had a recognisable smell - especially the coalman who carried sacks of coal to tip into the cupboard under the stairs where we kept it. Another garden memory relates to my job of collecting, with my little bucket and spade, the horse's droppings for my daddy to put on the roses. I remember that smell alright!

Our road was just off the Lea Bridge Road in Leyton. It was still in Essex then but is now in the London borough of Waltham Forest. The smells of that road are so evocative of my childhood. At one end stood the gasworks, which had a smell of its own - a mixture of burnt coal and gas. We played in the street every day after school and the gasworks had walls with ledges half way up - ideal for bouncing balls at as they rebounded really well. We played many games like Hide and Seek, Hop Scotch, Whip and Top Jacks and dressing up. We didn't always have a whip and top but used the tops from ginger beer bottles and home made whips.

Although I did sometimes wonder whether if a bomb hit the gas holder at the bottom of our garden there would be a big bang, I had no realisation that we could be hurt by such an event. At the other end of the street, was Potter and Moore's factory which produced soaps and talc and such like. I loved to sniff the air as I went past. I remember seeing Gracie Fields when she came to open the factory. The road had been re-tarred and I, being quite young, was taken up the road by some of the 'big girls'. Unfortunately, my mum had dressed me in white socks and shoes and I did not know about tar being sticky! I seem to remember trouble.

One most important smell was my 'fishy' bag. In the late thirtie, my father's aunts had a boarding house at Westcliff - then a popular holiday venue for Londoners - and we often went there. Now my daddy liked winkles and another of my jobs, when the shrimp and winkle man came round on Sunday's, was to winkle the edible part from the shell with a pin and I had this woven grassy bag that must have contained shrimps or winkles. It was green and pink and smelt lovely, or I thought so then. A good reminder of my daddy at home. He left us when I was six.

When I started school, I had to go across the fields which were part of Leyton marshes. I remember my mother taking me on the first day (I was not quite five) and being annoyed that she wanted to come in with me. Mostly, I remember being taken to school by the 'big girls' who were probably nine or ten years old. I'm not sure that would happen today.

There was a large area of grass and a little stream and a footpath from Church Road down to the railway. You could go over the bridge or down under a tunnel to get to the other side. I loved to scream in mock fear when the steam trains went rushing by with that lovely enginey firey smell. Before the war, there were swings, a roundabout and other play equipment there but when the war came they were taken down for scrap metal to make guns and aeroplanes and other weapons and a large piece of the grass was dug up and bomb shelters built - for the factory workers, I assume. Our play was much enhanced by a huge bomb crater where the swings had been. The thrill of running down one side and seeing how far one could go up the other must be rather like skateboarding today. On our route we passed over the little stream on a bridge and then walked up to the school beside the wall of the Wireworks. The smell of that stream is still with me. It was clear with sticklebacks near our play area but, under the bridge, it was oily, browny-green, sludgy and very pungent. Also on that walk, we passed rows of lovely May Trees and Privet Hedges. I always remember those days if I smell Privet.

Tastes are something else that prompt my memory. On occasional Sunday afternoons, I was taken on the Number 38 bus to Chingford. The bus that took us on those outings had the stairs (I always had to ride on top) on the outside!

From the Royal Forest hotel, we could walk into Epping Forest. I remember a certain 'Lemon Ice' - it was about four or five inches long and triangular and you pushed it up in its tube. The taste of that gorgeous confection was heavenly. I have longed to taste it again. The nearest I have come to it is lemon sorbet. Recently I was there in Chingford and everything is much the same but there is no ice-cream man on a bike with a box on the front and the words 'Stop me and buy one' written on it.

A less happy memory was of a holiday in Babbacombe in the wartime. For some reason my mother had gone out, leaving me with the landlady of the house where we were staying. A really bad thing for a child to do in those days was to "not eat up your food". Now this good lady had made a rice pudding for me. It was not like my mum's however - all creamy and delicious - but plain, boiled, unsweetened rice and I hated it. I have to admit I was not always the most biddable of children and I would not eat this rice. Stalemate ensued. I sat at that table for what seemed like hours till my mum came back. Somehow she sorted the problem out but the landlady never forgave me. I had wasted precious, rationed food and committed a crime in her eyes.

Food was scarce during the war but I do not remember being hungry. Without my dad at home, we had one and a half ration books but we seemed to manage well because I had school dinners and Uncle Arthur, my godfather, ran two allotments which supplied us with fresh fruit and vegetables. We did go to the British Restaurant some times and I remember the lovely jam roly-poly with custard that they sold. Also, I had a Mars Bar each Saturday evening and I cut it into eight pieces and made it last all evening if I was careful.

Another favourite of mine was to put a spoonful of sugar and the same of cocoa powder in to a paper bag and shake it up. Then I would wet a finger, dip it in and suck – this could taste even better if I was able to add a spoonful of powdered milk. My best treat was scrambled egg made with dried egg powder.

One of my favourite outings when I was very little was to go to London on some Sundays to visit Lyon's Corner House in Tottenham Court Road. I always had to have baked beans on toast - my favourite. One time (I must have been four) when walking along the road up there, I suddenly lost my daddy. It was the most dreadful feeling I had ever had. Then I saw him, ran up to him and grabbed his hand. But when I looked up, it wasn't my dad! Shock...horror and a very bad feeling in my stomach. My dad turned up just in time but that feeling lasted all day and the worst of it was I couldn't eat my baked beans. Not a nice memory that.

Sounds also have the power to recall those days. The most vivid being the sound of an aeroplane at night when I am in bed. I still lie and hold my breath while planes pass and I put this down to the air raids that I experienced as a child. There is no doubt that my clearest memories relate to noises. The raids themselves were so noisy - with guns booming, bombs dropping, bullets pinging and, later in the war, the doodlebugs buzzing before the awful silence that led up to the load explosions. Yet I never had any conception that I could come to any harm, even though I knew people sometimes had, and I have no memory of the adults around me being afraid so I was not afraid either.

It was the noise of the plane and the metallic sound of its bullets hitting the road that makes the memory of Babbacombe so strong. We had just come off the beach area when my mother pulled me under a hedge and made me lie still. The lady from the house called us to run in but mum said no. Then I looked up, saw a plane low above us and heard the bullets ricocheting along the road. I could see the pilot who had a helmet and goggles on and, at age seven, this became my image of a German. He went as quickly as he had come and I quickly realised why people referred to this as a 'hit and run' raid. The enemy planes flew in, dropped bombs, shot at people and then left as quickly as they had come. Some days later I developed German Measles and, being in a boarding house, had to go into the local isolation hospital and really believed the German had shot them at me (such is a child's logic). Actually, the recent raid had been bad and bombs dropped on the tennis courts and the beach had killed several people.

I have one very clear memory of coming home in a car - a rare event - and then being in the hall of the house when a loud wailing started up. I clung to my daddy's knees in surprise. "What's that?" I asked. I was told it was the siren. "What does it mean?" I asked and the reply was "The bad men are coming!" Thus, although I did not realise it at the time, this became the beginning of a few momentous years in our house. I have never forgotten that morning.
But many sounds bring back happy thoughts. I loved the radio (no television then) and associate it with good times like sitting in the tin bath on Thursday nights in the living room listening to Tommy Handley, a comedian, who with his fellow actors made us laugh about the Germans and the war by creating characters with funny catch phrases and voices. I loved the variety acts and serials of 'Monday Night at Eight O'Clock' and 'The Happidrome' and the music - especially 'Worker's Playtime'. I sang a lot when I was a child and was encouraged to do so for I had a good voice. The sound of singing as we sat in the air raid shelters gave me a love of community singing - and the old songs from World War One and the Music Halls can take me back again. My dad had a good tenor voice and the happiest sound of all was hearing him singing to me when I was put to bed - old songs like 'Drake Is In His Hammock' and 'Go To Sleep My Babby'.

The sights that trigger memories are from a world where there were fewer cars on the roads, we played in the street quite safely and I was very small. All I remember of my grandfather is a long pair of legs going up and up and, at the top, a gold watch chain and I definitely remember standing on tip-toe to look onto the table top. We had an old-fashioned style dresser in the living room and the lower half was covered by a curtain. This was my den until I became too big to fit in it. The little girl from upstairs and I would sit under there and drink cocoa with much slurping and saying "soup of the evening - beautiful soup" with gales of laughter.

I was a rather sickly child and often needed a fire in the bedroom at night. Although there was a coal fireplace, usually the oil stove was lit. It was a black cylindrical shape with a disc on top that could be open or closed. When it was open, it was magical because the pattern on the lid was projected onto the ceiling. If the fire was lit, the flames made beautiful dancing patterns round the room but nothing was as good as the oil stove patterns.

I think I have always loved gardens. My earliest memories are of yellow tea roses and tall delphiniums and helping my dad in the garden. My job was to collect snails in my little bucket but dad drowned them which I did not like!

Christmas was lovely with candles on the tree. I still have some of my parents' decorations from 1928 when they set up their first home. We put them out every year.
A great treat was when the magic lantern was lit. If you

opened a little door on the side there was a little oil lamp that provided the light source and slides that were passed in front of the lens. There was quite a variety but I liked the Disney ones best. The coloured pictures were shown on the wall and the operator told the story that we saw unfolding. I thought it truly was magic!

We had two windows in our living room each divided into upper and lower windows and, during the raids, three of the sections were shattered at various times. We came in from the shelter one Christmas morning to see the broken glass all around again. There amidst it all was a beautiful doll leaning in its box against the table leg. I really believed it had survived the raid though logic now tells me it had been placed there after the raid by my mum. I never thought that Father Christmas couldn't get through the planes and barrage balloons!

Another time, we took a trip to Bognor Regis on a crowded train and I noticed there were many uniformed passengers. I had looked forward to going on the beach. Imagine my disappointment when I saw barbed wire all along the road blocking any access to the sands.

Of course there was always bomb damage to be seen but bomb sites with their ruins were good playgrounds to children and became 'cowboy lands' and 'fighting the Germans territory' fuelling our imaginations greatly. I had a lucky escape when playing 'Germans and English' for a boy poked a stick in my face and narrowly missed my eye. I had several stitches in my eyebrow.

Pictures In My Mind

Although it was towards the end of the war, and I was nearly ten, the most significant event I can remember was being taken by my mother to the pictures and seeing the footage of the concentration camps. The people running the cinema had given clients the option of leaving before the footage was shown and returning to see the rest of the programme afterwards. My mother believed I should see it. Although, at that age, I did not understand the enormity of it all I shall never forget those images.

It is only natural that, because I was a young child, I have no memories of the struggle that everyday life was for the adults in my life. But the incidents that I do remember have left their mark in subtle ways. It was Wordsworth who said, "The child is father of the man" - a saying I have never really understood until now.

So, Elizabeth, I want you to understand that I did have a happy childhood despite the difficult times. I was loved and cherished just like you. I played with my friends, had parties and went to school though it was a different world. And talking of parties, I am reminded of one last picture. It was my birthday party and my mum had made a cake. Now, she had found a recipe for icing made from, among others things, powdered milk. It did not look too bad but, when my mum came to cut it, it was SOLID. In the end, the icing was broken into lumps and we all sucked our bits. It tasted lovely and caused a lot of laughs. May you survive to a good old age and have many happy memories of your childhood too.

A Window on My Life

To My Mother

By Margaret O'Regan

My story begins early in 1936 - the year that King George V died. I remember this well as, a few weeks after he died, my father died. He died of a heart attack which was the result of inhaling mustard gas during the First World War which weakened his heart.

I was four years old when my father died while my brothers were ten and eight - my mother was only thirty-seven. She had been ten years younger than my father. Her widow's pension was ten shillings for herself, five shillings for my eldest brother and three shillings for my younger brother and me. We could have been put in to a children's home but my mother wouldn't let us go, even though she knew that life was going to be a great struggle. There was no income supplement or children's allowance in those days - only free school boots for my brothers once a year, and free school dinners.

As it was nearly impossible to live on this kind of money, my mother had to go out to work. I should point out that, if you did try to get some extra help, you were told to sell parts of your home. I was allowed to start school before I was five so my mother could work during school hours and, if she was able to get more work after school hours, I would go with her. So, for no other reason than the hours suited her, my mum became a charlady – and, without today's domestic appliances, I can assure you this was not easy work. She washed other people's clothes, scrubbed floors (no fitted carpets or vacuum cleaners) and did all the other dirty jobs no-one else wanted to do. Added to this, mum had to keep her own house clean and bring up us three children which included making sure we kept out of trouble. But it didn't take long for us to learn that her word was 'law' and, if we stepped out of line, we would soon know about it. My brothers would run errands for neighbours to earn some pocket money. Times were hard but my mother never complained and always seemed to find some time for us kids. Some of the people my mother worked for were kind and gave my mother things for me, such as their children's clothes as they grew out of them. I didn't mind that they were second hand and never really thought about them being someone else's cast-offs. I was really happy to have the dresses as they were copies of Shirley Temple clothes and she was a big child film star at the time.

Well, time passed and over the next three years we moved house twice – I was too young to remember why. Then, in September 1939, war broke out bringing more problems. We lived in Ilford on the outer edge of London, so all the schools were closed and most of the children were evacuated. My brothers went away for a few weeks but didn't like it so they came home and my mother decided we would all stick together. The schools didn't open again until after the war ended so the only schooling we had was for half a day a few days each week in different houses. This didn't last long, however, as very few children attended so it was decided it wasn't worth the bother.

Life went on as usual for a while because the war didn't affect us for a long time The Blitz, as it was to become known, didn't start until the middle of 1940. At this stage,

we hadn't been given an air-raid shelter so we had to go
each night to the local park shelter. My mother had acquired
from somewhere a large wooden barrow and this was
packed with bed clothes for us to sleep in. Each night, we
would push the barrow to the shelter and in the morning
push it home again. After a while, my mother got fed up
with doing this so we just stayed at home and took our
chances. It was September 1940 when the bombing started
and then we really knew there was a war.

We didn't live far from a large park where there was a
gun battery stationed and, as soon as the sirens were
sounded to warn people to take cover wherever they could
because the German planes were on their way, these guns
would start firing to shoot down the planes as they came
over the Channel. There was also a gun on a lorry that went
round the streets to try to get any stray planes that got
through.

Things really got bad and one night, in particular, stands
out in my mind; there was a mass bombing on London and
all around where I lived. We had five families in our house -
it seemed that everyone who was in trouble always came to
my mother but that was my mother, always ready to help
anyone even though some were better off than she was.
There had been two nights when we were all evacuated
from our house because there were some unexploded bombs
that could explode at any time. This wasn't any hardship for
us kids - we thought it was a bit of an adventure, going out
in the middle of the night and watching the planes overhead.
We didn't know if the planes were ours or the Germans' and
we were too young to realise the danger we were in.

Obviously my mother was well aware of the danger and she must have been worried out of her life. The worst night of the Blitz, then, for me – and one that I remember very well - was the mass bombing of London including all the docks, the Tate and Lyle sugar factory as well as many houses. A lot of people were killed that night. When we looked towards London from where we lived, the sky was a bright red from the glow of all the fires. There were air raids most nights and bombs fell all around where we lived and I'm sure my mother felt very relieved to find that we were all still safe each morning but, thinking back, I don't think us children realised just how lucky we were.

At this point I must tell you that my mother, my brother and myself all did a paper round first thing in the morning and then, when we were finished, we would have breakfast and my brother would go and help one of the milkmen and I would go and help the milk girl. By this time, I was about eleven years old and remember this as one of the happiest times of my life. I learned to drive a horse and cart and earned myself plenty of pocket money which meant I could buy things for myself and my mother that she couldn't afford. Every time my brother and I went out, my mother would say, "If the warning goes, knock at any door and they will take you in". We agreed (to stop mum worrying) but, needless to say, we never did knock on anyone's door.

Life went on like this for many months and, by this time, my eldest brother was working in a butchers shop. This was very handy as the butcher would give my brother pieces of meat and sausages that were going spare which helped given the meagre rations that we were allowed. He worked there for a long time but eventually got fed up with it and left. He then got himself a job as a driver's mate with a firm called Carter Paterson which delivered goods all over the country (this was long before the company became British Road Services). He stayed there for many years and eventually my younger brother joined him. This left my mother and I on our own most of the time as they were often on long distance runs and were sometimes away for two or three days at a time.

We were eventually given a Morrison Shelter which was basicallya huge iron table with metal grills on the sides to stop the debris from falling on us if the house was bombed. It was set up in the downstairs front room and included a mattress to sleep on. We also had a bed in the room for my mother and I to sleep on until the air raid warning started (sometimes we were lucky and there wouldn't be a raid, but not often). This suited me as I could roll out of one bed and into another, taking our dog with me to cover him up to stop him barking when the raid started. Once again, looking back, I now know it wasn't so good for my mother. She would beg me not to go to sleep and keep her company as, by this time, she was worrying about my brothers. She often had no idea where they were or if they were in danger but, within minutes, I would be asleep leaving her to worry alone.

Next, in 1944, came the V1 flying bombs soon to become known as 'Doodlebugs'. These were bombs that had wings and flames coming out of the back end of them and they flew without a pilot. If one of these stopped flying only once it was over your area, there was no need to worry as it would land and explode away from your house. On the other hand, if a 'Doodlebug' stopped overhead, you had to make a quick dive for cover with the hope that it wouldn't land on your house. Once the powers that be realised what these 'Doodlebugs' were, the gunners would do their best to shoot them down as they came over the Channel.

After this came the most deadly weapon of all – the V2 rocket; it was a silent bomb and nobody knew it was coming until it came down and exploded. There is no need for me to say as you will have by now guessed that this thing caused a great deal of damage and many people lost their lives.

To everyone's relief, 1945 saw the end of the six years of war and for the next few weeks there was celebrations every where. Best of all were the street parties for us children - how people managed to get the food together I really don't know but they did somehow.

Later on in her life, my mother became very stressful. I was about sixteen and, like all teenagers, not very tolerant which meant that we didn't get on at all well and were always arguing. I got married when I was eighteen and left home but still kept in close contact with my mother because, for all our disagreements, we still loved each other.

A year later, I had my first baby and my mother was 'over the moon' with joy. By this time, I had gone back home to live because houses were very hard to get to rent and we could not afford to buy one. The big advantage, however, was that we had a built in babysitter – mum!

Eighteen months later, I then had a little girl and this completed my mother's happiness. We now had what she called 'a pigeon pair'. We still didn't get on very well but, as long as mum had the grandchildren, she was more than happy. In her eyes, they could do no wrong but my husband and I could do no right.

Sadly, my mother became very ill when she was sixty and she was in and out of hospital for many months (for years she'd had badly ulcerated legs). She never recovered from her illness and died aged sixty-one.

After she died, I began to realise that I was the reason we had not got on in later years. It had been my fault more than hers. With children of my own, I now knew why she was so short tempered. Having brought up three children with very little money, the worry of the war, and taking on everyone else's worries, her nerves were shattered. I should have known this and done more for her. She was one of the best, and would do anything for me or anyone else.

I wish to dedicate this story to my mother.

A Window on My Life

86

A Small Boy Goes To War

By Ben Paterson

The summer holidays seemed to go on for ever and ever. We had spent a month or six weeks in the usual house we rented in Sandown, Isle of Wight. It was a beautiful summer; that last one in peacetime. All packed up, Father had gone back to London, the luggage had been collected and sent 'passenger luggage in advance'(PLA). Mother decided to take my younger brother and I to Wiltshire to visit old friends from her Oxford days. It was the end of August. I knew we could not stay long as I was due to go to my preparatory school in mid September. New clothes had to be bought, labelled and packed in a new school trunk. All to be purchased at Daniel Neal 'School Outfitters' of Regent Street, London.

Thus it was that on the 3rd September 1939 I was in Alderholt, a tiny Wiltshire village a few miles to the south of Salisbury. We were staying with the Rector and his family. The Third was a Sunday. We were in church. Because the Prime Minister was due to speak on the wireless to the nation at eleven o'clock, the Rector had brought a wireless into the church. We listened to that broadcast. Even now, sixty-five years on, I get a tingling at the back of the neck when I hear Neville Chamberlain say the words "I have to tell you that no such undertaking has been given. Consequently, a state of war will exist between our two countries from midnight tonight". We finished the service.

The Rector read the prayer "to be said in time of war" - a prayer I was to hear every day for the next five years. As we came out of church, I noticed my father, who had come down from London for the weekend, talking to a young man of about nineteen. The conversation was becoming heated. We could not hear what was being said. Suddenly my father let fly with his right fist, caught the young man on the chin and sent him sprawling on the ground. Father turned away and came towards us. He was angry; it was the only time I ever saw him like that. Mother asked what the argument had been about. Father said quietly that the "boy" was a conscientious objector and had said there were no circumstances in which he would take up a weapon "not even to defend my family". It was this that caused the outburst. Father, who had served in France in the First World War, said the "boy" didn't know what the Boche was capable of doing. "The only good Boche is a dead one." A phrase I was to hear later many times. It was time to return home. We left the next day, catching the little train from Alderholt Halt to take us on its single line to connect at Salisbury with the main line.

The shopping for uniform took up most of the week. I was due to go away on the 18th of September. On the Wednesday of that shopping week, a letter from the school announced term would start on the 12th September. Panic! But, amazingly, all the new uniform, already labelled, arrived in its trunk. I added a few personal effects, locked the trunk, asked the railway to collect it for PLA and prayed that it would arrive in time. It arrived the day after my arrival. Looking back, I do not think we ever doubted its arrival.

On the 12th I joined the school train at Paddington – the 1.45 p.m. I have used that train many times since that first time. In later years I sat in the dining car; one could have lunch between Paddington and Oxford without having to rush! But not that first time. There were several new boys waiting to board the train all eyeing each other, but not talking; each one with his own thoughts. I seem to remember mine centred on whether any of them would help me fix my Eton collar to my shirt – and was the stiff starched collar going to make my neck sore. It did until one got used to it.

We were all handed over to the Matron after tearful farewells. At Oxford we were piled into a fleet of taxis, each one of us clutching a small overnight case. I still have mine, battered but serviceable. We were driven to Brewer Street to The Cathedral Choir School. That first night was strange; six small boys in a dormitory terrified of taking off their clothes in front of strangers. I suppose we must have got into pyjamas eventually. In later years we thought nothing of stripping off completely and leaping into the river Cherwell. Naked swimming took place at the all male bathing place called 'Parsons' Pleasure'. The whole area was surrounded by green painted corrugated iron sheets. Close by was 'Dames' Delight'. This was for ladies and children; costumes were worn at this bathing station. As the water was quite shallow our non-swimmers learnt to swim there before graduating to the deeper water next door!

There was no school that first week. Our job was to fill sandbags. This was a new experience for all of us. It was tiring to start, but it was fun and we all enjoyed doing it.

College staff built walls of sandbags around entrances, and in front of street level windows using the bags we had filled. We filled sand bags in the morning. After lunch, the younger boys had a rest on their beds. Then we went to the school's playing fields in Christ Church Meadows to play pick up football. Back for high tea, a quiet period of reading or letter writing, and bed. We, the nine year olds, were in bed at seven o'clock; lights out and no talking half an hour later.

It was a small school. In the previous three terms the number of boys had risen from sixteen to twenty-six. My intake's arrival brought the official number up to thirty-two plus three refugees the Headmaster had rescued from Germany and Austria during his summer holiday. Our numbers now meant we could play eleven-a-side games. The year before, the teams were eight a side, providing no one was ill. This was not unusual as choir schools only catered for choristers. Westminster Abbey, St Paul's Cathedral and Canterbury had bigger choirs and our great rival King's Cambridge was gradually building its numbers to twenty choristers plus probationers.

That first term was one of finding one's feet, following the example of the older boys. From the very start we knew what was happening in the world outside. The main news was read by the Headmaster from The Times at breakfast as we ate our cereals and toast. He did this throughout the war, occasionally offering a comment. His comments, particularly about North Africa, usually had a classical connotation. "Hannibal came from there" or "St Paul was shipwrecked on Malta".

All the windows in the school had brown sticky paper criss-crossed on every pane of glass, and there were blackout curtains throughout the school. It would have been impossible to black out the cathedral. Evensong was sung at five o'clock each day. Actually it started at five past five, according to the tradition that allowed canons who were fishing in the river to pack up and get into the Cathedral in time. As the days drew in, the Dean and Chapter decided to move Evensong back to three o'clock; it remained like that until the end of the war. This change meant that games, played every day, had to be moved to later in the afternoon. In the winter, games were played on Saturday mornings.

But the winter of 1939-40 was a severe one. Christmas time was one of the choir's busiest in the year. We sang our Carol Service of Nine Lessons on Boxing Day so were unable to start our Christmas holidays until after that. We actually finished formal schoolwork just before Christmas. Traditionally after that it was party time! The Dean's party, The Master of Chorister's party, the Headmaster's and so on. Although there was rationing at this time it was not as restricted as it was to become later; there was no shortage of food. All the party givers had children of their own and the tables were stacked. The food on the tables quickly disappeared. The boys gave the impression they had never had a square meal in their lives. Games were played. The most popular was 'murder in the dark' followed by 'sardines'. These went on for ages because of the enormous number of rooms in the great houses in Tom Quad.

We went home for the holidays and another Christmas. My parents had decided to move out of London. We went to the supposed safety of Guildford. It seemed a short holiday, but it did start to snow. Back to school. We had just arrived at the station when I realised that I had left my ticket, ID card and ration book at home. Luckily our temporary house was not far from the station. I ran home to collect the documents, and ran back to the station just as the guard was blowing the whistle. Mother had kept the door open and I flung myself into the carriage as the train started to move. I took a long time to get my breath back.

It snowed. Oxford had at least a foot of snow. Walking from school across to Christ Church was an effort. Gradually we had worn a track for ourselves, but it soon became icy and very slippery. On one occasion crossing St Aldgate's we saw a policeman on the other side of the street. One of us, who shall be nameless but became a very distinguished author, decided to throw a snowball at the poor man. It hit him on the back of the neck. The consequences were dire. The perpetrator was marched off to the police station after service. We were told he had received one stroke of the birch. True or not, it was a salutary lesson. The rest of us were "gated" for a week and there were extra lessons.

Spring came. Dunkirk happened at the end of May. Many of the troops evacuated from the beaches came to Oxford. There were a number of hospitals and rehabilitation centres round the city. The patients in their bright blue suits with white shirts and scarlet ties were a common sight in the Oxford streets. The call-up of men to the forces meant that all the adult members of the choir of military age left to be replaced by undergraduates on

Sundays only. Two undergraduates that were to become familiar faces on stages across the world livened up Sunday services. The longest service in the Book of Common Prayer is the 'Ordination of Priests and Deacons'. On a good day with about ten priests and deacons to ordain, the service would last about three hours. A test of a small boy's bladder! The main part of the service took place at the High Altar with the choir way back in the Nave. Not many people took any notice of what the choir was doing so long as it sang on time and in tune. It was easy for our two undergraduates to have a bit of a party! One of them had bought a tin of Mackintoshes' 'Quality Street' to the party. Each of them had half of the tin from which they proceeded to throw toffees across the aisle. The choristers' slip catching improved that summer! The congregation, not many of them at our end of the Cathedral, probably thought we were trying to catch mosquitoes or flies. On weekdays, Evensong was sung by the boys only.

After the awful winter, we had a long hot summer. For reasons I never understood the family gave up being evacuees and returned to our own home. It was during these summer holidays that the Battle of Britain was fought. It seemed to be fought immediately over our south London house. For a lot of the time my brother and I used to lie in the garden gazing up at the sky. It was madness really. Shrapnel and spent cartridges used to shower down on the garden. We collected it all and by the end of the holidays had quite a collection.

One Saturday afternoon when my parents were round at the church hall rehearsing a sketch my father had written for a church get-together, we were in our usual place in the garden when we saw a Messerschmidt 109 coming straight at us with all its machine guns firing. We leapt up and dashed to the garden shed that was to one side of the garden. There was a loud roar of engine and sounds of glass being broken. Then silence. We stayed in the shed for some time; it was probably no more than five minutes. When we came out we saw that all the windows on the ground floor at the back of the house had been smashed. Wow! Here was an opportunity to collect bullets that had really been fired at us. We started looking. But at that moment our parents returned. They had heard the commotion and wondered whether we were safe. They couldn't believe what they saw and were certain we had gone on a wild rampage. Not that we had ever done so before. It was only when I pointed to a bullet lodged in the sideboard that they realised we were telling the truth. For my mother that was enough. We had to pack our bags, arrange for furniture to be collected and put into a repository, find a house in Oxford and move there quickly. This we did.

There was one strange stroke of fate. After we had left London, my father who had had to remain because of his job, joined the Auxiliary Fire Service. He had served in France, Gallipoli, and Greece being wounded several times but not sufficiently seriously to stop him joining the Indian Army in 1919. In 1922 he was seriously wounded on the North West frontier and evacuated back to England. When he was fit, he had to resign his commission and was not put on the Reserve. In 1939, he had tried to rejoin the Army, but was turned down. The fire service was his way of "doing his bit". The winter of 1940/41 saw the start of night bombing raids on London and elsewhere. His detachment of two engines was called to a fire in a furniture repository in south London. My father realised that it was the repository where all our furniture was stored. When the team arrived it was obvious that they could not save the building. All our furniture was destroyed except a grandfather clock and some pictures.

So for the rest of the war, and in fact until the early sixties, we lived in Oxford. When I returned to school for the autumn term an enormous and formidable air raid shelter had been built above ground outside the school's backdoor. It had rows and rows of bunks, decent lighting and heating, folding tables and chairs and chemical loos. Although we frequently spent the night "in the shelter", it never had to be used as a classroom. Many years later it became the dayboys' cloakroom and changing room.

That first year was exciting for two reasons; it was a new school with all that that implies, and it was the start of a war that to us nine year olds was fun with its maps of front lines and lists of ships engaged in battles. The father of one of the choristers was in 'HMS Devonshire' at the Battle of the River Plate. We played war games; learnt about the French and Petain, and the withdrawal to Dunkirk and the British generals Gort and Ismay. Our war games entitled us to award each other medal ribbons. Strangely like those who lived their lives in the Underground shelters, the very different existence in our grand shelter brought us more closely together. A not to be forgotten experience.

Oxford was never bombed even though the Cowley works were building aircraft and their engines. It was always said that Oxford and Cambridge would not be bombed if similar treatment was accorded to Göttingen, Heidelberg and Tıbingen. Maybe, but it was also said that Oxford was covered in a mist from the river that could not be penetrated by bomb sights. Bombs fell on Cumnor Hill about five miles away but they were jettisoned by an RAF Wellington trying to get back safely to Abingdon.

We grew up quickly in that first year of the war. The scouts and cubs were taught first aid including artificial respiration. We were taught elementary cooking when rations allowed. We had fire drills using stirrup pumps and practised throwing sand from buckets on to imaginary incendiary bombs. We learnt how to join broken wire safely and to repair fuses. Our tutor was a parent, a distinguished German professor, who was later to write about the buildings of every county in England. On Sunday evenings we listened to records from the Headmaster's vast collection in our pyjamas before we went up to bed. He loved Schubert songs, many of which he sang beautifully. It was all great fun.

Oh joy! That in our embers
Is something that doth live,
That nature yet remembers
What was so fugitive!
The thought of our past years doth breed
Perpetual benediction.

Holiday Job

By Arthur Razzell

It all started after the death of my father. I was just fifteen, at school and needed a holiday job to help myself and my widowed mother.

It so happened that I sang in the local church choir and had a friend Bill who sang tenor with me. Bill had for a number of years been running his own small building firm and offered me just the right job as a general helper.

In those days Bill would find a plot of land and get an interested client to buy it. Bill would then agree the requirements of the client in terms of how many bedrooms, what bathroom equipment was required (such as bath, shower attachment, toilet) and how the house was to be heated. Even in quite expensive houses, central heating was not so usual but hot air heating from the back of the lounge fire to the upstairs bedrooms was being tried out. Bill would then design the house and get the planning permission from the local council.

Work would then begin and the first job I had was to clear the house site of nettles so that the shape of the house could be pegged out. I had to help dig the footings. These were only two feet deep and about eighteen inches across and not at all like today's which are up to two metres deep and reinforced with steel rods. I was glad we were to build on solid chalk as it meant it was easy to get a firm footing. After this Joe, the full time handy man for Bill, gave me a choice. Either I could fill the cement mixer or I could wheel barrow the heavy wet concrete to the footings. I thought I would choose the easier option of filling the mixer. Unfortunately Joe could wheel the barrow far faster than I could feed the mixer, so he had several breathers while I kept at it. By now the summer holidays were over and I was off back to school.

I watched each weekend over the next few months as the house took shape. First came the Birch Brothers - father and six sons - all brick layers. The first job the family did was to dig the trenches and lay the drains for the house. Father and the eldest son then built up the corners of the walls while the middle sons laid the bricks in between. The younger boys, not much older than myself, mixed the mortar and carried the bricks for the others to lay. They put up their own scaffolding; no specialist firm being called in as would happen today.

Next Bill and Joe built the roof as Bill was the carpenter. No prefabricated roof trusses; only long lengths of nine inch by two inch timber or four by two's for other parts. First the wall plates which were timbers along the top of the brick work were cemented in place. The beams to hold up the upstairs room ceilings were then nailed in place with six inch long nails. After this the rafters were cut to shape and length before being nailed to both the wall plate and the beams at the wall end and to the ridge board at the top. Because of so much timber cutting, this job could take a week or more to complete especially if there were dormer windows to be fitted.

Next a firm called Redland Tiles would arrive to tile the roof. Bill never tiled a roof himself as breakages of tiles would be too expensive. Meanwhile Bill was making the staircase in his workshop back at the yard. This was a hand crafted piece of woodwork with no machinery used, only hand tools. Back on site came the Birch Brothers to plaster the walls, followed by the Brown Brothers for the plumbing and Taylor's to do all the electrical wiring.

Next on the scene came Arthur, the second of Bill's workmen. Arthur was a professional house painter and decorator. His first job was to prepare all the surfaces for painting. This involved hours of sandpapering and filling of nail holes with putty. After this every visible knot was treated with liquid knotting before the first of several undercoats was applied. It was nothing unusual for wooden surfaces to have at least a primer, two undercoats and two top coats of paint. The walls would have two coats of porous distemper to allow the walls to dry out. No dry lining in those days.

As far as I can remember the new owners were responsible for the gardens and so, with the house finished, the owner could move in to put up their own curtains etc. and start sorting out the garden.

The next summer Bill offered me more holiday work but this time on another new house. This one was in the stages of being finished off and I had the job of helping Arthur rub down and fill the staircase. I had never realized how many nail holes there were in a staircase! The job seemed to me to go on forever. However, after a while at this site, I met 'Bill Number Two'. 'Bill Number One' had no lorry of his own to transport away rubble or bring sand to the site while 'Bill

Number Two' ran a carter's business from his home in the High Street and helped the team in this way.

Now it so happened that the two Bills and my Uncle Sid had all sung together as boys in the choir that Bill and I sang in. Each day at ten o'clock we all stopped for a break. It was often at this time that 'Bill Number Two' would join us and start yarning about his youth. These stories enchanted me as I knew several of the characters in the stories.

Bill Number 2's father had also been a carter in the 'Depression' and Bill would tell tales of how his father would take a horse and wagon, loaded with wooden scaffold poles and barrels for the sand, up Wimbledon Hill followed by men running on foot or riding on bicycles asking him where he was taking the poles. Each was seeking employment at a very difficult time in the 1920s.

Bill Number Two's father would walk the ten miles to Croydon in the late afternoon each Saturday and, when Bill was very young, would buy the boy a pair of shoes. Whatever he brought back, Bill had to wear. We would all be scandalized if we heard of parents doing this today! Bill's father would also wait until the butcher's was just closing at about 8 o'clock each Friday evening. This was the time that the butcher reduced the price of the meat as he had no refrigerator or cold store to keep the meat in over the weekend. Likewise, in Surrey Street Market, the price of vegetables and fruit were all being reduced. Loaded down with the meat and vegetables, Bill's father would then walk the ten miles back home. How many fathers today would do

this every weekend to enable the family to eat?
Bill Number Two also told me that many children at his
school never went home to lunch because there was nothing
to eat at home. Bill also remembers going home at
lunchtime to be given a jam jar and told to go onto the
common to collect blackberries. He would take these back
home for his mother to stew up with (if they were lucky) a
spot of sugar and that would be Bill's whole lunch. My great
grandfather was the caretaker at the local infant and junior
school and, in the worst of these winters, would provide
soup and bread free of charge to the very poorest children.
He paid for this out of his own pocket; his wife making
both the soup and the bread.

'Captain French' and 'General Pop Pom' were both
elderly members of the same choir my Uncle Sid and the
two Bills belonged to. Now it is said that General Pom Pom
got his name from the choir boys because he sang base and
his singing used to sound like 'pom pom, pom pom'.
Captain French was the local blacksmith and the Captain of
the Fire Brigade. Now the fire engine was kept in a garage
type building at the bottom of the High Street. It was a
horse drawn machine and, if there was a call out or practise
run, the first job was to catch the horse. The horse was kept
in Coolin's (the corn and coal merchant) field about half a
mile from the fire station. Two men would run, or ride their
bicycles, to the field carrying a halter. Sometimes the horse
would come to them but, on other occasions, it would
gallop to the far end of the field and then fun and games
would start to catch the beast. The standing joke was, "Send
a message to the fire to tell it to keep going until we get
there!".

Like all young people of that day and age, these children had to make their own fun. T.V. and Game Boys were still to come so children played skipping, ball games, 'Hoop and Stick' as well as 'Five Stones', 'Hop Scotch' etc. Sometimes they would play 'Knock Down Ginger' as well as 'Please Jack May We Cross the Water?' and other games that did not need equipment. But this did not mean the children were always good. On one sunny Sunday morning after church, the choirboys went across the fields to a pond next to which was a pigsty. The boys took off the door to the pigsty and put it on the pond as a raft. Out came the farmer shouting blue murder at the boys who immediately paddled to the middle of the pond. Out came the pigs from the sty and off went the farmer to catch them. After this the boys then paddled to the side of the pond farthest from the farmer and ran off home.

Bill Number Two was very amusing and a great story-teller but one thing he would never do was put on a collar and tie and thus he never went to his daughter's School Parent's Evening or Prize Giving even though she won many school prizes. He is somebody that I remember, however, with great affection. It was Bill Number Two who named me 'Professor' as he knew I wanted to go into the sixth form and go on to teach.

Bill Number One (the carpenter) then offered me a job for a third year and this time I helped build the roof of a bungalow. This particular summer was very wet and the wood we had delivered was saturated. This made it very heavy to carry and difficult to cut. It slowed the

construction down but we did manage it in the end.
So ended my glimpse into the building trade. What I learnt
by practical experience has stood me in good stead in later
life and I thoroughly enjoyed myself. How I regret that
today's young people are so restricted in what they can
experience due to such things as Health and Safety and
Employment Law!

A Thirties Christmas And Beyond

By Primrose Razzell

My childhood was not spent in Maldon where we live now but in Caterham in the county of Surrey on the top of the North Downs. The beginning of November was the time for at least one visit from children lugging round an old pram containing a home made guy with an ugly red cardboard face. Their pleas of "Penny for the Guy, Missis" left my mother stony-hearted although, as she used to say, "Carol singers are a different matter". I noticed that my mother was still fairly stony-hearted if the carol singers arrived in early December, but she melted as the days went by and in the week before Christmas every group of children who arrived on the front doorstep would receive some coppers. Mostly the carol singers would consist of a couple of ten or eleven-year-olds with two or three younger ones in tow. They would sometimes sing part of 'Away in a Manger' or the first verse of 'Hark the Herald Angels' before they banged on the door but far more usually it would be a few verses of the Sans Day Carol which was undoubtedly the local speciality. I have learned since that this was not, as I imagined, taught in the local primary schools but was quite possibly harking back to a time when carols were handed down by word-of-mouth.

My grandmother used to visit us nearly every day and, at the end of November, she would say, "It's nearly Stir Up Sunday; its time to make the Christmas pudding!" The raisins that she used in the pudding mix were large Smyrna ones and contained seeds which she removed by pinching the raison flat and holding it up to the light in order to see the seeds and remove them easily. Christmas decorations were never put up in our house before Christmas Eve afternoon. My mother, my brother Martin and I went out into the local wood armed with thick gloves and clippers to cut the holly and bring it home; we would stick it behind the pictures and put it into the two polished brass shell cases that my father had brought home from the Great War. The Christmas tree grew at the end of the garden all year and was dug up and brought indoors in an old tin bucket on Christmas Eve. The bucket was tastefully hidden from view during the twelve days of the Christmas season by a piece of red crepe paper. We had a box of pretty coloured glass balls and tinsel which came out year after year to decorate the tree. There was a silver star for the top of the tree and an angel with a white crepe paper dress trimmed with more tinsel. There was also a little celluloid man with a smart suit and wobbly eyes which delighted us. The cheap set of Japanese tree lights worked rather intermittently and annoyed our father!

Christmas Day began long before daylight when my brother and I began exploring the excitingly lumpy stockings at the ends of our beds. Back then time seemed to speed up and the rest of the day went almost in a flash; Christmas hymns in church in the morning, the special chicken at lunchtime and the blue flaming brandy on the pudding seemed only five minutes before we were welcoming in the aunts, uncles and cousins for a Christmas party tea followed by games and charades. Before we knew it, our guests would then leave, calling out their 'goodbyes' in the cold air underneath the misty halo of the gas street lamp. Then a few days later, it was Twelfth Night when all the cards were taken down, the holly was carefully burned on the sitting room fire and the tree re-planted in the frosty garden. Goodbye Christmas 'till next year!

The events of September 1939, however, brought a change to the peaceful domestic routines around which our lives had been built up until that time.

Our house was in the danger areas which circled both Caterham Guards Barracks and Kenley Aerodrome which was the home of a fighter squadron. In 1940, our house was requisitioned as the cook house for a hundred soldiers. The cooking was done on my mother's brand new gas stove and the gas company fitter who cleaned and renovated it eighteen months later said that it had aged ten years! The cooks lived in our house and served out the meals for the hundred French Canadian soldiers. The soldiers suffered from the cold in our damp, chilly, English winter. Although used to cold, the dry Canadian cold did not bother them as much as the English version of cold. Some of the houses where they were billeted lost their internal doors and some furniture in their efforts to keep warm but, as our gas stove was on all day every day, I expect that our house was warmer than most of the others and thus stayed in one piece.

When our family left Caterham, we went ten miles away to stay at Tadworth with our aunt Grace and uncle Howard and cousin Marguarite. Margie is seven years older than I am and it was good to have another girl to play with although I think I must have been a bit of a trial – I remember on one occasion chasing her round the garden with a dead minnow in my hand and trying to put it down her neck!

On the journey from Caterham to Tadworth my mother, my brother and I went by train. I suppose that the Battle of Britain was taking place at that time for we could see from the train window that the sky was criss-crossed with smoke trails and small silver aircraft were circling each other. There were many sudden puffs of grey smoke too and we could hear constant distant explosions. Our train stopped in a railway cutting for some time before continuing to Tadworth.

We lived at Tadworth for eighteen months and part of the time was spent in a house my father rented from a doctor who had gone into the army. I remember particularly that that winter (1940) was notable for the fact that there were several inches of snow on Christmas Day. On another occasion, we had 'black snow' in our garden. I picked up a piece and I could see printed writing on it. Later on we heard that one of the big London libraries had been bombed and set on fire. The ash had been carried high into the air by the north wind and settled in our Tadworth garden.

In 1942, we were able to go back home to Caterham. While we had been at Tadworth, we had often seen a great orange glow in the sky to the north. This was caused by the burning of the many bombed buildings in London. We could clearly hear the German bombers going over our house in Caterham after the siren at the end of the road had given its up-and-down wailing warning but, by 1942, they only seemed to come at night. My father had made a dug-out shelter at the end of our garden but, due to our garden being on clay soil, this filled up to the brim with crystal clear water and so was no use to anybody! Our family, instead, crammed into the cupboard under the stairs which we were assured was the safest place in the house. For a few weeks, we also had great aunt Ada from Highgate in London to stay as her house had been bomb damaged. I thought that she was a rather grim old lady but no doubt she'd experienced enough to make her look grim. My grandmother also came to stay for a while and I had to share my bed with her. I was (yet again) rather a trial and fidgeted a good deal so, although the double bed held both of us quite comfortably, I was always getting told to keep still.

On another occasion, one of the German bombers shed its cargo of small incendiary bombs over Caterham. Two landed in our garden, one landed in the road outside and the Congregational Church in Caterham Valley was burned out. The head mistress of my school had a narrow escape that night. The school had a number of boarders at that time and she had to get up at night each time the siren went off to take these children to the school shelter until the 'all clear' sounded. The Congregational Church was on the opposite side of the road from the school and she did not get back to bed that night. When she arrived back at her bedroom in the school, she found that an incendiary bomb had come through the roof, through her pillow and bed, through the floor and ceiling of the room below and fortunately burned itself out on the concrete floor without setting the school on fire.

Gradually the night raids petered out but, in 1944, the flying bombs (V1s) began. The 'buzz bombs', as they were called, looked like small aircraft with squared off wings and a small spurt of fire coming out at the back. They made a horrible grating roar as they went across the sky but nobody seemed particularly scared of them – providing the noise and the spurt of fire were there. When the noise/fire stopped, however, it was time to take cover (if you could) as the 'buzz bomb' would be falling out of the sky and the large explosion that followed could knock down half a dozen houses.

The flying bombs were aimed at London but they also fell on the North Downs. Barrage balloons were tethered along the Downs and it was hoped that they would entangle the bombs so that they would explode harmlessly in open country. If they did, the blast would make the fins on all the nearby balloons flap about as if they were clapping their hands in applause!

My father worked at Sydenham so he went off to work by train quite early in the morning but, one April - shortly after my tenth birthday, the rest of us had a nasty surprise at about 8.30 am. A V1 had fallen in the next road to us and demolished three bungalows. It had killed a nine-year-old boy and some soldiers who were in a Jeep. The windows of our house had blown through and the bomb had damaged our roof so that you could stand in the hallway and see blue sky through the hole. It had brought down the lath and plaster ceilings in several rooms and my mother and small brother (who were nearest to the blast at the back of the house) suffered injuries. My mother had a badly cut lip and head from the flying window glass while my brother had bruises from the pieces of ceiling plaster falling on to him. I had been awake but still in bed at the front of the house as my school did not open 'till ten o'clock that day. I had not heard the explosion but did feel a violent shaking of the air in my room and broken glass landed all over the bed. I carefully tipped the broken glass out of my shoes and put them on before my mother came in. Her face was steaming with blood but she was very calm and told me to get dressed. The road warden, Mr Wightwick, soon came and my brother and I were taken to their house at the other end of the road while my mother was taken to the doctor. Her cuts healed quickly but six weeks later a piece of glass finally found its way out of her scalp! Mrs Wightwick gave us all cups of very sugary tea which was considered good for people in shock. Later that day, we went to stay with the two Miss Smiths and their elderly father. They had cellars under their house and we all slept there for about a fortnight. My father stayed at Tadworth with his sister Grace's family as our house was uninhabitable. This was the beginning of the summer of 1944 when my mother, my brother and I led an almost refugee life.

After saying 'goodbye' to the Smith family, we three went to Digswell in Hertfordshire to stay with my mother's school friend, Marjorie Burn, and her family. They lived in a

large house with a little wood in the garden where we
picked wild strawberries for tea. Old Mr Burn showed me
his stamp collection and Marjorie played ball with us. Three
weeks later, we were off again for a six week stay on a farm
at Henley-in-Arden, Warwickshire. The mixed farm was
owned by uncle Archie and auntie Wyn who were friends of
my grandmother. They had a daughter about my age called
Janet and the three of us used to play all day in the fine
summer weather. I fed the hens, rode on the tractor and
rode on 'Drift' the cart-horse. Drift and I 'helped' with the
milking and the hay-making. They had a land girl working
on the farm and I decided then and there that that was my
future career too!

Soon it was time to leave by train for Westmorland
where we were to stay near the village of Great Asby on
another farm owned by my father's cousin Annie Sowerby
and her husband George. The journey was hot and very
slow; it involved changing trains several times and, during
one such change, we missed our train completely. We were
then put on another train full of sailors going back to their
ship in the Clyde. At one stop, the W.V.S. were serving them
cups of tea - except that the 'cups' were empty jam jars as
the proper ones had run out. On the train we had become
friendly with a family called Steele who lived at Penrith. Mr
Steele discovered that it would be impossible for the three of
us to get nearer to Great Asby that night, so we all got off
at Penrith. He then took us to the only hotel in the area but,
unfortunately, the smart lady who answered the door said
they were full. So Mr and Mrs Steele took us home and, by
doubling up their four children, managed to give us
somewhere to sleep. I shall never forget their wonderful

kindness to my tired mother and her two grimy children. The next day we caught a train to Appleby where uncle George picked us up in his car. He was allowed a small petrol ration as he was a farmer.

We lived at 'Fell Close Farm' for three months with George, Annie, Sally (George's sister) and great aunt Maggie who was Annie's mother and very old indeed. She sat by the fire in the living room when she was well enough and, on one occasion, taught me the Victorian art of curling feathers with a knife. Annie cooked on the open fire which also heated a tank of water on one side and had two ovens (hot and cooler) on the other side. Oil lamps provided light but water was no longer dipped out of the well in the garden; it had been piped to the house a fortnight before we arrived. There was no other house visible from Fell Close; just the rain swept, open fells of the High Pennines. The fields were enclosed in dry stone walls and there were black faced sheep and small brown cattle in them. There was a rabbit warren in one field and George set snares there. We had rabbit for dinner several times each week. Annie made butter and cheese, bread, bacon and sausages. There was always plenty of milk to drink and we had rice or tapioca pudding nearly every day.

All this suggests that life was comfortable and quite cosy but it rained for at least part of every day for the entire three months that we were there so everything was always slightly damp. The rats had their 'dance floor' above our bedroom, so to keep them quiet, we had to kneel up on the feather mattress bed and knock on the low ceiling. There was a little stone built shed behind the farm house and inside was a wooden bench seat with two holes which were covered by wooden lids. This was the privy but it did not smell as Annie scrubbed the seat and tipped down Jeyes Fluid every day. My brother and I walked a mile to the Great Asby Primary School. The hefty local children did not think much of these skinny southerners but we made friends and all enjoyed picking apples in the school garden and basking in the warmth of the big coke fired stove (lit at the end of October) in the school room.

One day a letter arrived from my father to say that the War Damage Commission had completed the repairs to our house so George took us to Appleby Station early one morning. Annie provided us with sandwiches - but also butter, a cheese and sausages to supplement the wartime rations back in Surrey together with china to replace the plates and cups smashed by the 'buzz bomb'. Our house certainly had been mended but, a few years later, the back wall began to fall out and had to be rebuilt. Also, the ceilings were never as strong as before and a couple fell down one night. All this lay in the future after the ending of the war in 1945.

On V.E. (Victory in Europe) night, there was an enormous bonfire on the Green at the end of our road. The grown-ups were chatting and laughing and we children ran round and round the fire till we were all dizzy under a clear star-lit sky. Later, there was V.J. (Victory over Japan) night but, although there was a bonfire, it also rained and everyone seemed quieter and more thoughtful. I think people had begun to feel that, although the war was over, the future was likely to be darker, more uncertain and much less rosy than it had been during our early dreams of peace. Rationing went on for another seven years and London, plus many other towns, had been deeply scarred by bomb-sites. I was eleven in 1945 and, for me, the ending of the war simply meant 'no more hiding in the cupboard under the stairs'!

A Window on My Life

A Wren
In The Rigging

By Jo Robson

Paddington Station was bustling with passengers and a bunch of Marines were spilling onto the platform as I climbed on board the smart new diesel train. Jokingly they said what a shame it was that my 'sister' wasn't coming too and then helped me put my holdall up on the rack and made way for me to get to the window and wave 'goodbye' to my mother.

I was on my way to report to H.M.S. Dauntless - the training establishment for the WRNS. At Reading station I was met by a Naval tilly van, and ferried the half hour journey to Burghfield along with a dozen other raw recruits - all destined to spend the next month finding out if we were what the Navy was looking for.

Those first weeks flew by with us learning quickly how to fit into a completely new way of life. Labelled a 'Provisional Wren', I was issued my uniform. This consisted of a navy blue serge skirt two inches below the knees, a matching jacket, a white cotton shirt, a black tie and stockings with flat lace-up shoes and topped off with a flat white wren's hat with the name of the establishment in gold on a navy ribbon. I was glad of my great coat in the cold winter but hated lugging it about on other occasions when it was too hot to wear – it weighed a ton! There were also the 'unmentionables' known throughout the forces as 'passion killers' - elastic topped and bottomed knickers.

117

I shared a room with a Yorkshire lass, who I only ever remember as 'Yorky'. Our intake had been put into divisions like army platoons and I was in 'Thesius Division' where I learnt to march and lay out my kit. We were up at the crack of dawn, woken with a tannoy call of 'Wakey, wakey, rise and shine', and given chores to do around the compound before lessons and lectures throughout the day. This was basic training and we worked hard. We did have a weekly run ashore into Reading. Dean Martin and Jerry Lewis were favourites at the cinema and, while waiting for transport back to camp, we treated ourselves to hot-dogs or burgers at the station stand. However, we were horrified to hear a couple of weeks later that the very same hot-dog stand owner had been accused of using dog food in his burgers. I was relieved that I had stuck to the hot-dogs but some of my oppos were not so lucky.

The first month flew by and, having chosen our future category or job, we then signed on the dotted line agreeing to serve for four years of our young lives. It was my eighteenth birthday on the 17th December 1956 and, coincidentally, the Director of the WRNS' birthday too. She was to take the salute at our passing out parade and so I got a special handshake before we all went home on leave for Christmas.

Having been proudly shown around the family in my uniform, I went off to Wetherby in Yorkshire for my Part II training. Here I learned all I needed to know for my new role as a naval shorthand writer. I never quite came to terms with my arm badge - a blue 'ST' (presumably for 'stenographer') would have been an embarrassment for any girl and it became the butt of many jokes. Each month we had a free issue of sanitary towels or 'bunnies' as we called them while the naval ratings were issued with free condoms and a rum ration or 'grog' for those under age. Needless to say we didn't receive these other items. I had been brought up with a fair amount of naval jargon, my dad being a Chief PO Telegraphist during the war. Now I had to learn the relevant shorthand short forms and official procedures, as well as having endless speed tests.

We worked hard for four weeks, and when we did get a run ashore it was just down into Wetherby, a small market town; grey stone houses, a few shops and a couple of pubs. Here I had my first ever view of the yorkshire moors hitherto only read about in books like Wuthering Heights. Once we went into Leeds which I found grimy and oppressive – it was as I had imagined the industrial north to be. I missed Kent and felt homesick for the first time.

We worked hard with speed tests every day. The standard grey Olympic typewriters clattered away after dictation and we pushed ourselves to new heights. Occasionally, we had a break - like a hockey match against the young naval rookies we shared the camp with. The laugh was they played left handed to give us poor girls a chance - and still they won the game!

The ceremonies of 'raising the colours' at nine in the morning, and taking them down again at sunset, are well-known daily procedures on any military or naval establishment - both on land and at sea. If you were caught anywhere in sight of the flag mast at these times, the procedure was to stand facing the mast and salute for the duration of the ceremony. Consequently, everyone would duck into the nearest door to escape 'facing the mast' if in the vicinity at these times. On one of these occasions, several of us had ducked into a door and, because we were jostling inside the doorway, we managed to set off a fire extinguisher which had been inadvertently left uncapped. The result was an explosion of bodies from the building - screaming and laughing and violating the sacred silence of the 'sunset' ceremony. We were all put on report and brought up before the Officer of the Day next morning with an extra kit muster and cancelled shore leave as our not unreasonable punishment.

After the final tests and passing out parade, we were officially in the Women's Royal Naval Service and lost our 'provisional' status. My first posting was to St. Budeaux in Devon and what I didn't know until I got there was that I was to be a Marine Wren.

Having arrived and settled into my hut dormitory in Wrens' Quarters on my first morning, I was piped to the Reg. Office where a smart black official car was waiting to take me to Stonehouse Barracks in Devonport. I was so nervous because this was a whole new ball game. My hat was fitted with a sparkling brass badge, which I had to clean, instead of the ship's name ribbon. I was now about to learn another set of rules. The nicest thing was I was the only wren in barracks and, therefore, treated like a princess. My boss was the ADC to the Major General and next to my small office was an even smaller office in which my saviour and friend worked - Nobby Clark. He was a civilian in charge of all the mail but, like a dad, always had time for me and helped me out of many a hole.

On my first day, I reckon every marine in barracks must have dropped by to see what I was like. I must have been acceptable and had loads of invites to join all sorts of activities. Nobby became my protector; I was very naive and still wet behind the ears to most things.

The work was OK. I was used to the uniforms of the Coldstream Guards when I worked in Whitehall for the WD Land Department. That had been my first job after leaving school and I had been well used to marching feet and bands but all this paled into insignificance once I joined the Marine barracks. The practising for Beating the Retreat, and other ceremonial occasions, were a daily event on the parade ground outside my window and I was quick to appreciate their immaculate performance.

I did miss the company of other wrens though and rarely saw another woman. Some of the officers had their living quarters on the perimeter of the main Barrack Square. One particular officer was Captain James Edwards, his wife Caroline and three-year-old son Mark. With a young brother at home, I was well used to looking after a small boy and had baby-sat since my early teens. It was, therefore, with no worries that I agreed to baby sit for the Edwards. Mark was no problem at all but, unfortunately, his dad could well have become one.

Returning me to St. Budeaux, sometimes with a late pass, the Captain would stop the car outside the gate and scrabble in his pocket for some change, which I always found embarrassing. On one of these occasions, he'd obviously had a few too many to drink. There was no drink and drive rule then. He reeled towards me begging for a little 'kissy' but I was out before he had time to get out of the car. I had boyfriends and kissing was no problem but I was still a virgin and I did not want to open any doors for a married man and officer who was really my employer.

Whether this incident had anything to do with what happened next or not (I never knew), within weeks I was transferred to work in the Commander-in-Chief's office in naval barracks. I swapped my distinguished marine hat badge for an HMS Impregnable ribbon with mixed feelings. I was sorry to leave marine barracks, but it was nice to be one of the rest of the girls. I had missed out on a lot of fun.

It could have been like any other office job had it not been for my 'special assignments'. As a shorthand writer, I had to take notes at court martials and boards of enquiry. One memorable enquiry was on board HMS Puma, a Jaguar class frigate. I was collected each day by an official car (like being back in Marine Barracks) except we went into HM Dockyard and I was delivered on board the ship. One enquiry was into an incident which bordered on an act of mutiny and was considered very serious.

The proceedings took place in the officers' mess and I was allocated the First Lieutenant's cabin to type my notes back. Alone, and surrounded by what must have been more than a hundred elephants of all shapes and sizes (Jimmy the One's private collection), I was looked after by a couple of ratings. With mugs of tea and coffee flowing, they also had to stand guard outside the 'heads' whilst I 'spent a penny'. There were no wrens on ship's compliments at that time, and no female facilities - all very embarrassing.

The Captain had a double-barrelled name and a wife who was a lady-in-waiting to the Queen. He was a charming man and put me at my ease, introducing me to my first real curry. His cabin, where we had lunch, was full of polished brass and leather and I wished all my jobs had been so luxurious.

There were several other enquiries and one Court Martial (which was a lot more formal) but this made for a more interesting job.

Plymouth was just a bus ride away and I often palled up with a bunch in my dorm to go to the Naafi which was a good place to meet boys and dance. It was probably the best NAAFI I ever came across during my service and was strategically placed on the edge of Plymouth Hoe. We had a lot of laughs and always a string of dates. I learnt to drink Babysham with the best of them and then we got in with some PE Instructors. We accompanied them to rugby matches, not that I ever knew the intricacies of the game. On the coach on the way back from matches, we girls would all feign sleep and shut our ears to the words of the songs they sang.

We swam a lot too but I was never any good - I just couldn't do the crawl. I was brought up believing nice girls hung on to their 'halfpennies' until they got married but I was desperate to be one of the girls. All the girls wore Tampax which meant they could swim any time of the month and I was determined to do the same. Unfortunately, however, I didn't read the instructions properly and ended up in sick bay having been unable to sit down. Of course I hadn't removed the cardboard casing so, as well as suffering some sort of toxic reaction, I had to learn how to be one of the girls the hard way - even if they did all think it was hilarious.

Another memorable occasion was the Queen's Birthday Parade on Plymouth Hoe. We had all been amassed at the Citadel and, once in our platoons, marched in a parade around the bends that wind up the Hoe to the main stand where I understand Drake once played bowls and spotted the Armada. The WRNS platoon was so placed that we were between two bands - the naval band and that of the Somerset Light Infantry - each with different beats. This meant each time we rounded a bend we were out of step and chaos ensued.

The last straw, and one which reduced us to hysterics, was when we finally came to a halt and were standing to attention. We were right opposite the canons that fired the twenty-one gun salute so we braced ourselves for a big bang only to find they were mostly blanks. However, once we'd relaxed, a few live shots were fired and we all jumped out of our skins. Public onlookers were quick to see the funny side, and we didn't have a snowball's chance in hell against just one contagious laugh. Thank heavens it was only the rehearsal and the actual day went much better.

I learnt to sail, crewing whalers and cutters, and developed the love I had always had of the sea. I did some amazing expeditionary training on Dartmoor where we met up, by design, with a group of Dutch matlots visiting the port. We ended up in Princetown in an awesome rendezvous with our transport outside the prison. I'd never seen a prison before and was struck with such a strange feeling of melancholia that reduced me to tears. Regardless of what the inmates had done, I could not visualise a worse place to be.

The Dutch ship laid on a dance for us and afterwards I wrote to Hans, a signalman, for several months. At one time I was writing to eight guys on different ships that had visited and invited us onboard at different times. Together with the local nurses, we were a quick sauce of acceptable female company for ships calling into the port. I found myself frequently thinking about what my father had warned me of when I first joined up. "Just comforts for the boys," he said. Reading between the lines, I knew that my father thought we would supply all the men's needs but it wasn't true. We had a lot of fun and were mostly treated with respect. Plymouth had, like every other port, its own 'red light' district. Whenever the US fleet were expected in port, I learnt that 'ladies of the night' were imported from near and far. It wasn't that this area was 'off limits' to us, we just didn't go there.

Being a peacetime wren was quite different to what I imagined it must have been like in the war. During our basic training one essential thing we had to do before being able to sign on was to wear a gas mask into an air-raid shelter.

Once inside, the door was shut and we were told to remove our gas mask and breathe in some sort of gas, probably only tear gas, but it certainly was frightening. Perhaps it proved we would take orders whenever, I wasn't sure, but anyone who didn't do it was out on their ear. That was the nearest I got to experiencing an act of war.

A huge US 'flat top' came in and we put on a dance for them and, in turn, were invited back to be entertained by them. I met an engineer called Donald Schaefer who was the spitting image of Dean Martin. We had several dates, but always in a crowd. We wrote for a short while but then my next posting came through and I decided to sever all my pen pals - life was getting too complicated.

We had some good parties in The Camel's Head in St. Budeaux. The best one was one of the girl's birthdays. We conspired to climb the majestic flag mast that dominated our quarters. This was where the young sparks and signalmen, who also lived on camp, did their training. Alas, when we returned to quarters, only one lass had the bottle to attempt the climb but she was spotted about 30 feet up and all the alarms went off. Someone had left his radio switched on and the message came out loud and clear over the entire establishment that there was "a frigging wren in the rigging".

I arrived in Londonderry, having crossed from Hailsham to Belfast, just as a 'burning bogie' filled with straw had been sent into the station with a political message from the IRA. Confused and scared, I waited for an hour before my train was allowed to disgorge its passengers and found a familiar tilly waiting to take me across the Foyle to HMS Sea Eagle - the Joint Anti-Submarine School on the outskirts of 'Derry'.

Here I worked hard and thoroughly enjoyed a completely new job. The work covered all sorts of experiences. I took notes for the Navy at a huge civil Board of Enquiry where a young rating on guard had tragically killed his best friend. The poor chap was devastated as it had all been a hideous accident. They had been fooling around like kids but his gun was for real and had been cocked. "Bang! You're dead!" the young rating had said, jokingly. But his friend really was dead. They were both under eighteen years of age.

Another enquiry related to a helicopter accident where the pilot had plunged into the Foyle estuary. The verdict was accidental death, and not mechanical failure, but there was the possibility of suicide. These enquiries began to get to me and, after a few months, religion crept into my life.

Being a much smaller establishment than Devonport Barracks, the wrens were a close- knit few. I joined Lynne, a writer, in the Main Office. She was very enthusiastic about a forthcoming visit from the evangelist Billy Graham. There was to be a big convention and I got swept along with her enthusiasm. Lynne had a scooter and I rode pillion with her to the convention. It was before helmets were obligatory and the nearest thing to riding in an open sports car with the wind blowing through your hair. The road to Port Rush was like a roller coaster and we used to try to get a good head of speed up the first hill, then switch off the petrol, and glide down and up the next few hills as far as we could. The trouble is, when the petrol is switched off, so is the control and we nearly didn't make the convention at all. The convention was certainly an experience and Lynne went up to the stage to say she had seen the light but I'm afraid I didn't. I always had been a bit of a rebel, and something inborn stopped me in my tracks.

Being from a joint forces school, I again joined up with the marines and learnt to canoe on Loch Neigh. The Air Force had a station not far up the road and it was there that I took the exam to become a Leading Wren or 'killick'. Since I passed the exam, I suppose people had come to feel that I had at last settled down and could be trusted with responsibilities.

I loved Ireland, and so determined to see more of it. Three of us bought ourselves bikes and, on days off, cycled around the surrounding breathtaking countryside. For our next leave, instead of going home, Ann, Monica and myself took the train to Dublin and then cycled the road around southern Eire. We spent the first night in the YMCA by mistake, with a chair under the doorknob - our only security. The hostel charge took the form of a menial chore and mine was to polish the ominous brass front door knocker.

The next day, the weather was blistering and poor Ann was very fair-skinned and ginger-headed. We camped by a river and thought we might have to take her back to Dublin if she was going to get sun-stroke. Later the same day, we woke in the middle of the night to find a bright patch of light shining at the foot of our tent. The light turned out to be moon-light reflected on the water seen clearly through a hole which had been chewed by water rats that were after our bread. Lesson learnt, we bought a container for any tempting food and where possible hung it from a tree.

Ann recovered overnight miraculously and the next day we cut down our mileage from sixty to fifty miles, with panniers laden; it wasn't too bad. In Galway, we were accosted by an irate priest telling us to cover our legs so we each bought skirts having only brought shorts with us. Other than that, we never had a threatening word the whole trip, although we had been warned back in Derry not to broadcast that we were in the British Forces. The locals were always very friendly and I'm sure bright enough to put two and two together. We were English and living in Derry. We ate at communal tables in various roadside inns, laughed a lot and enjoyed different company and drank in the wonderful countryside to Killarney and back to Dublin. Back in Derry they thought we had been somewhere really exotic abroad, with our beautiful tans.

Too soon my next posting was to the NATO Exercise Office in Portsmouth. The WRNS quarters were in Southsea - old and dilapidated buildings that should have been pulled down years before. Here I had my twenty-first birthday, away from home, but my Mum had sent me a small cake and I met Rick, a Fleet Air Arm mechanic. A small Naafi club across the road from our quarters was a breathing space to relax and smooch with jukebox favourites like Blueberry Hill and Lonnie Donegan's skiffle group. When the exercises were over, I did a stint in the C-in-C's office when I met up with my only nasty piece of work during my

entire service. The man was a particularly slimy Naval Chief
PO Writer who piled a load of reports on my desk and
ordered me to make myself acquainted with their contents. I
was by then pretty experienced with most sides of naval life
and thought I could handle whatever came my way. I'd seen
Mess Decks on board ships at Christmas full of blown-up
condoms with painted faces and not batted an eyelid but
what I was about to see was very different. I saw reports on
incidents that had happened on board various ships relating
to cases that were, I'm sure, not meant to be seen by a
female – I read about sodomy and other perversions I
previously knew nothing about. I felt revolted and was
physically sick. The Chief quite obviously revelled in my
embarrassment. For the first time, I requested to see my
C.O. and asked for a transfer. The man had made my skin
crawl and certainly got to me.

Rick and I had become pretty serious and, on my next
leave, I spent some time with him at his married sister's
home in the Midlands before taking him home to meet my
parents. We got engaged and then I got my posting to
Chatham. I was pleased because Chatham had been my
Dad's home base. I never wanted to return to Pompey,
which differed to my other postings which had provided
fond and happy memories.

I worked as secretary to Lt. Commander Derek Ford. He
was an absolute sweetie. A bachelor in his mid-forties and a
real gentleman. We got on like a 'house on fire' and I
introduced him to the joys of Johnny Mathis on my portable
record player one afternoon. I remember his huge blue eyes
rolling to the ceiling as my favourite singer hit his highest

note in 'Misty'. The Commander was in charge of NATO exercise orders and I had to run off hundreds of copies on the ancient and inky duplicator. Oh for today's copiers! Minutes of meetings, exercise orders and various reports all had to be collated by hand, complete with rubber finger stool, around a huge conference table. A back-breaking job. I worked nights in the underground Operations Room during exercises, trailing doggedly around after my boss, taking notes, with the plotters busy following the participants. Emerging into the fresh air of an early morning, or sometimes late at night when the rest of the world was asleep, all made for a completely different work experience and I loved it.

Wren's quarters were in nissan huts at the far end of the barracks. We had a small entrance from where we could take a short cut around the allotments and into Chatham which is where I started to take driving lessons. The driving school had a fleet of Morris Minors and was a great way of getting to know the area taking in Gillingham, Rochester and even Faversham. This part of Kent I had never been to. Although I had been born in Folkestone, and had been taken hop-picking as a tiny baby, the war then broke out.

I was lucky enough to be excused parades, that is all parades except the monthly pay parade. That was down in one of the huge sheds in the dockyard where most of my fellow wrens worked. We also had open Navy Days when all the family could visit and the public were allowed on the ships alongside. We had a fun marathon and I nearly killed myself running a couple of miles on concrete roads (plimsolls just weren't made like the trainers of today) and I suffered horribly from cramps.

Rick and I met whenever we could as my four years service slid gently to an end. Thoughts of a Spring wedding obliterated any possibility of re-signing on the dotted line, although Rick could be sent to sea at an time. It had all been a brilliant experience and four years of my life I will never forget.

Precious Moments

By Pat Sizer

As a child I had riches. This, however, is a paradoxical statement; my father had very little money. The gift I received from him in abundance – and far more precious than money - was his time. Sadly this is a commodity that some modern children have to go without or receive very little of. It is, of course, the most valuable thing their parents can give them.

I was born and grew up in a small village in Gloucestershire. Our valley was one of the five radiating from the town of Stroud. When Queen Victoria passed through it one Autumn, she called it the Golden Valley. Although not as tourist-ridden as Stow-on-the-Wold or the Slaughters, it is every bit as beautiful.

Our house was the middle one in a terrace of five, built in the year of Queen Victoria's Jubilee and named Jubilee Crescent. In my early childhood, none of these houses had running water. This had to be obtained from a communal tap in a small backyard that ran between the house-backs and the brick-built wash-houses. Our wash-house contained a brick copper for heating water, a pile of coal in one partitioned-off area and my mother's iron mangle with big wooden rollers. On a tall wooden bench was the galvanised washing tub and scrubbing board. In a walled-off section with a separate door was the box lavatory. We were luckier than some villagers since our part of the village was linked to a sewer and the lavatories could be flushed by pulling a high chain. As a small child, I had to stand on the side of the box in order to reach the chain handle. In inclement weather it also meant we had only a three-yard dash across the paving to the toilet, while other poor folk had an unpleasant trek up or down a long garden path to the privy. All the children in the terrace were forbidden to play with the tap in the yard but, as it was closest to our back door, the temptation was too great for me to bear. The tap produced a variety of fascinating noises, depending on how far you turned the handle; the water splashed and then glugged and gurgled as it ran down the drain. If you inserted your thumb in the tap end you could make the water squirt all around in a most appealing way. Great fun! Wet feet mattered not a jot; playing with the tap was irresistible.

One day, when my mother's back was turned, I indulged my enthusiasm for water play at the tap when a sudden, loud and alarming noise seemed to fall down from the sky. I paused in my pastime and gazed up but the frightening noise went on, only to be accompanied by a sudden scream from my mother who dashed out, grabbed me under one arm and ran back inside the house. To my utter consternation and amazement she thrust me under the table and told me to remain there. I did. Whether my infant brain questioned mother's sanity at the time I do not recall but seconds later she joined me there, scrambling under and remaining there until the noise ceased and was followed by a different sound at which point we both climbed out. It must have been a year or so before I realised the noise was an air raid siren, followed by an 'all-clear'.

The back door of the house led directly, down a step, into our kitchen with its old-fashioned black range (shiny from its encounter with my mother wielding the black-leading brushes) which was surrounded by a black wire fire-guard with a brass top which I liked to rub with Brasso to make it gleam like gold. Our only light came from a hissing gas mantle set into the wall above the range. When I was able to stand on a chair, I found out how easy it was to poke a hole in the fragile gas mantle by simply touching it very gently with a spent match. I must have cost my parents a fortune in gas mantles. What a little monster I was!

The kitchen floor was made of uneven stone slabs and, from there, you went down another step into a small passage which lead past the pantry which was constructed in the space under the stairs. The brown pantry door had a white ceramic handle and inside there were all sorts of culinary treasures. There were jams, jellies, bottled fruit, pickles and chutneys, all gleaming like jewels in jars. A large galvanised bin contained a substance called isinglass in which my mother preserved eggs when there were any available. My grandparents lived only four miles away and kept chickens and bees, so we were better off than many people for eggs and honey. Another interesting object to me was a large meat safe, made of wood with a pierced metal front, which must have let in air but kept out insects and any other pests that might have been lurking. It stood on a large, cold, marble slab which cooled and preserved all manner of things. Fridges were virtually unknown to ordinary working people.

But I'll close the mental door of the pantry and lift the latch on the living room door, which has a dimmer memory for me than the kitchen. In here was a tall mantelpiece around a coal fire and another gas mantle (less easy to poke holes in as it was set in the ceiling and therefore higher than the one in the kitchen). It was the front door, however, that I remember in great detail because a memory of that door caused me far more alarm than any air-raid siren.

Up until this time, I had been the only child living in the house. I was born three years after my mother had had a distressing still-birth so I was a much-longed-for baby when I arrived and duly looked after and protected with great care which will help to explain why what happened to me next was such a terrifying experience. As I shared my mother's room, there were two spare bedrooms in our house. Mother had been 'in service' before marriage and, therefore, had referred to both the upper and middle classes as the "gentry" for all of her life - a fact I found most irritating as a bolshy, arrogant adolescent. Anyway, when some kind of a voluntary social worker (probably from the middle classes) arrived enquiring as to how many bedrooms we had, the social worker's plummy accent proved enough to browbeat my mother into accepting four evacuees. All were boys; three from the east-end of London and all suffering from impetigo and head lice. The fourth boy was from Walton-on-the-Naze in Essex. I wonder if he is still alive and living in Essex? Each boy was over twelve and must have seemed like very noisy adults to a small, much protected toddler. I remember only two of their names, Peter and Terry, but only Peter still lives in my memory as he petrified me and the specific reason was connected with our front door.

A war-time rule that demanded the most strict adherence was the one regarding the black-out and requiring that all internal light remained hidden from the outside. All our windows had normal curtains and thick black ones in addition. Our front door was solid but there was a pane of glass above it so it, too, had a thick curtain which covered it from ceiling to floor. Strange though it may seem, this curtain remains my most vivid early memory. I can still see, feel and even smell it today. It was a dark rusty pink colour, thick, hairy and very scratchy when it brushed against your skin. When you stood near to it, or touched it, it emanated a hot dusty sort of smell which almost seemed to burn your nose. Anyway, it's in relation to this curtain that Peter became a terror. The curtain was not only thick but voluminous so you could stand behind it with your back pressed against the door without being noticed by anyone in the room and this is just what Peter did. He waited until I was alone in the room, having somehow positioned himself behind the curtain, and then when I went near it he poked his fingers into the curtain's voluminous folds and roared (in a deep growly voice) "I'm the bogey man and I'm coming to get you!"

The odd thing was I couldn't run away, despite being terrified. In fact 'petrified' is probably a more apt word; frozen to the spot! I screamed and screamed until my mother came running and I suppose, but can't recall, that Peter was soundly admonished. This telling off from mother did not prevent further performances, however, and only after I began to get bored with the same routine did Peter give up taking pleasure from my distress.

This period of time must have been so hard for my mother, especially with war-time restrictions and rationing.

There were no vacuum cleaners or washing machines and she was having to cope with four large boys after delousing them all and treating them for impetigo. I remember their purple faces painted with gentian violet, but not their features. Some months later, however, the boys were replaced with a young woman from Cornwall, sent to do war work at Gloucester Air Craft Factory. She was a farmer's daughter from Saltash and remained with us for many years which must have been nice for my mother as my father was away in the army for much of this time. She became a great friend and later, after the war, my little sister's Godmother.

It was in the evening and at weekends that my father gave me his time. The attention began when I was a baby with action rhymes like 'Ride a cock horse', 'This is the way the ladies ride' or 'Down to the bottom of the deep blue sea' which make most babies squeal with glee. Finger rhymes were added like 'Here is the church, here is the steeple...' with nursery rhymes, stories and poetry following on. By the time I went to school, I was positively addicted to books. Never in those early years did I go to bed without at least one story and some of these became my favourites. Poor Dad grew quite tired of reading 'Bindle's Wonderful Picture' and would sometimes 'inadvertently' miss this one out when reading the list from which I would make my selection. Sadly for him, I always noticed and that story had to be repeated. I expect he grew to recite it from memory and perhaps this was a good thing as all our reading had to be done by the light from one gas mantle - the only form of lighting we had downstairs. Upstairs, we only had candlelight and I well remember my mother's complaints about the number of candles I burnt while reading in bed at night. One evening, my little sister caused puzzlement when she demanded to be read 'the story about the farmer sticking a needle into his foot'. My father and I both searched a long time for this puzzling story request but to no avail. It was only when we were looking at a nursery rhyme book that she suddenly exclaimed, "That's the one!" She pointed to 'This is the house that Jack built'which contains that immortal line, "This is the farmer sowing his corn" and our problem was solved.

Books were the most important toy of my childhood, but I did have many others. Because of the war, attractive new toys were in very short supply. I was lucky that my father, goodness knows how, seemed to have all the right contacts enabling him to obtain good second hand toys. Looking back I remember being the only kid on the road, who had both a dolls' pram and a dolls' house. My few dolls were attractive china ones, not the ugly ones with composition head and rag body and limbs of wartime.

The road outside our house was merely a dirt track with no pavement or tarmac. The earth was very sandy and we played in it, very much like being on a beach. No-one seemed to come to any harm, so perhaps there is some truth in the recent report that today's children are not exposed to enough dirt to develop strong immune systems. The brick wall on the other side of the road had slate-coloured coving slabs on the top, which we used as mini blackboards for our colouring chalks, the latter also being used to put patterns on our spinning tops. When we had used up all the slabs we wiped some clean with a wet rag for re-use. No-one

complained about graffiti; I don't think anyone knew the
word and if a naughty boy wrote the occasional rude word
it was easily wiped off.

It was a sad moment when our creative efforts in the dirt
were ruined by the hooves of the huge cart-horse that pulled
the baker's wagon, carrying our bread delivery. This wagon
was just like the ones used by American pioneers travelling
west, as shown in the cowboy films we saw at Saturday
morning pictures - except the canvas covering on top was
black instead of white. Inside were massive square baskets
containing delicious-smelling, new-baked loaves.

There were two other deliveries by horse; one that pulled
a wide, flat, heavy cart which was owned by Mr Watkins
who delivered racy remarks along with greengrocery every
Tuesday and one containing several milk churns. Our milk
was rolled in its churn to our back door by the milkman in
his smock and leather gaiters and he would ladle out the
milk in pint or half pint measures into your waiting jug. If
you needed milk on a Sunday, you had to collect your own
from Farmer Bathe's farm about half a mile away.

Once school age was reached, it seemed as though the
outside world became our oyster. We were gradually
allowed the freedom of the fields, meadows and woods and
they wove themselves into the pattern of the rich tapestry
that was our childhood. With my father I picked flowers,
berries and nuts according to the season. He always seemed
to know where the very earliest white violets could be found
and where the largest blackberries grew, the latter a
welcome addition to our ration allowance. A welcome

pocket-money spinner was the picking of rose hips, for which we were paid a few pence at school, as part of a government health scheme. These were made into rose hip syrup, rich in vitamin C.

Another family activity, carried out by mothers and children, was 'wooding' – "Bist thee gwyin' woodin' with yer mam then?" you might be asked. "Giss us a bit o' thee rope and oi'l cum with thee." Armed with rope, we would search Park Wood for fallen dry branches which were tied together in bundles and dragged home to augment the coal ration.

In addition to fostering in me a love of books and a wide appreciation of natural history, my father also helped me to draw and paint. We would often make things together including woven mats from paper and rolled-up beads, dolls' house furniture using empty match boxes, walnut shells and conkers. Magic trees grew from folded and torn paper, as did rows of cut-out dancing girls. Miracles came from folding, cutting, moulding and sticking together - and from decorating with anything that came to hand. Unlike the sad comments sometimes heard today, I can't ever remember being bored. Can you see why I say I was rich in those days?

A Window on My Life

Knocking Off The Corners

(an excerpt from a full autobiography)
By Len Stephenson

At the beginning of the year I was working as a driver. I had started to get itchy feet, for I felt I was worth more money, and my boss said he could not afford to pay any more. This made me decide to hand in my notice and, in doing so, I learnt how good the old adage "Never throw away your dirty water until you have your clean" really was. My luck was in, however, since I had only been signing on at the Labour Exchange for about a week when I was interviewed for my first job.

One day the clerk said to me, "There's a gentleman in that office ready to interview chaps for a driving job". I knocked on the office door and entered before introducing myself. The man asked me several questions, and looked at my references, which luckily were first class. He then told me that the company he worked for was the household name, Ever Brothers Ltd. The job would be driving a van with a ladder on top and putting up posters on hoardings to advertise 'Life Buoy' and 'Lux' toilet soaps.

"Your companion will be a Superintendent and he will teach you the ropes," the man told me. He then asked if I was interested - the salary was to be three pounds a week – and I told him I most certainly was! This offer was 'manna from heaven' to me. "Well, good!" said the man. "Can you start today?" I replied that I would be very pleased to. "Excellent," he said. "Let's go and catch the train to Stratford and I'll introduce you to Jack Emberson who will be your Superintendent".

When we were on the train the interviewer (I'm afraid I have forgotten his name although he was a nice chap) asked me a few more questions and then asked to see my driving licence. Luckily, I had it with me and gave it to him. When he saw a speeding endorsement on the back he said, "I thought you told me that you had a clean licence?" I said that I was sorry but had thought that speeding did not count. The gentleman smiled wryly at this saying, "Well there's not much I can do about it now, is there?"

On arriving at Stratford Station, we were met by the Superintendent. Introductions were made and then my interviewer wished me luck, shook my hand and left us. How he had arranged to meet the superintendent at the station, I never knew. Anyway, Jack suggested that we have a cup of tea in a nearby café. "Jack's my name from now on, Len" he said and then we drove off in the van and I became a billposter.

Jack and I got on very well together and he taught me all about billposting; how to fold the posters and then, after putting the paste on the hoarding with a long-handled brush, how to position the poster before carefully unfolding it on to the board and brushing on to the paste. This was not easy to do in a strong wind, at the top of a high ladder, with a bucket of paste hanging from one of the rungs, but I soon learned to do it well.

Our work covered a fairly large area and Jack did not like driving much so he left it to me whenever he could. I well remember one fine and sunny day when we were returning from work at Southend-on-Sea. I had stopped the van. Jack was having a nice snooze with the passenger window down when a policeman rudely awakened him. I had been caught speeding again. For that I had to report to Bow Street Court, which I did by letter, and was fined two pounds before having my licence endorsed again. This time I did learn my lesson and I have never been caught speeding again since.

Meanwhile, while I was getting established in the business world, the political situation at home and abroad had been getting very bad. Hitler and his Nazi Party had been growing more and more strong and aggressive. It was quite obvious to any sane person that Britain would soon be at war with Germany. I had already joined the Territorial Army because of this and I was now in the 4th Battalion of the Essex Regiment.

I took two weeks leave from Ever Brothers to go on a fortnight's camp at Wannock. This proved to be great fun with long route marches, on which we sang the songs of the First World War. After all, it had only been about twenty years since the last war and some of the war veterans were officers and sergeants with us. We practiced bayonet fighting in mini-battles, firing blank cartridges and got as ready as we could for call up which we knew was to come soon.

My friend Gary had not been able to get a suitable job, so he had enlisted in the regular army and was now in the Grenadier Guards.

On September 1st 1939, Jack and I were working in South London when in the afternoon we saw on the placards outside newsagents the headline 'All members of the Territorial Army must report to their HQs at once!'

Without much ado, Jack and I got in the van and I drove as fast as I could to my home.

Saying goodbye to Jack, who seemed very upset as he drove away, I made my way indoors, changed into my uniform, kissed Mum farewell while she was in tears and reported to battalion HQ at the drill hall in Gordon Road, Ilford. There we were issued with rifles and bayonets, tin helmets and extra kit. Soon, we were ready to bed down. We kipped on the wooden floor, wrapped in the tow blankets each man had been issued with. We kept our uniforms on and used our boots covered with a towel for a pillow.

At Reveille we rose and washed and shaved in a hastily-erected ablutions tent. After breakfast we practiced bayonet fighting for a while and then we were allotted to our various platoons. I had not been consulted but still found myself in the Mortar Platoon. Not, as I soon found out, anything to do with cement but it was a platoon which could use a type of gun that fired three-inch mortar bombs.

A mortar is a two-inch or three-inch calibre metal barrel, secured to a heavy base-plate and held by a metal tripod. The barrel could be elevated by means of a handle on the tripod, and a sight for adjusting range was also attached. Mortar bombs were about fifteen inches long with ballistic

146

powder in the fins and could be slid down the barrel where it came on to a firing pin. This would propel the bomb a distance of 250 to 2000 yards. On exploding, it sent shrapnel up to a radius of 100 yards.

On the 3rd of September 1939, war was officially declared on Germany and we were in it for real. It was eerie at first because we did not get the heavy bombing which we had been told to expect. Little did we know then but poor civilians were enduring awful bombing and much devastation was left in its wake.

It was not long before we were told that the Battalion was moving to a secret destination. We had a short leave and then said a farewell to tearful wives, sweethearts and families. At HQ we piled into trucks and set off for the unknown.

To our chagrin and disgust we all finished up in Epping Town, about ten miles away. Here we debussed and were allotted billets, which had been commandeered. We did drills, bayonet practice and marching. The band and drums even found time to 'beat the retreat' on the village green. Our Colonel said that it was good for public morale.

Before long the Battalion was told again that we were moving to another secret location. This time we finished up in a town called Witham, another twenty miles away. We were getting fed up with this moving around and felt that it was not what we had enlisted for. Our platoon was billeted in an old manor house on the outskirts of town. We found some croquet kit in one of the rooms and, despite the cold, we were able to play some games on the lawn. Quite near us was a very nice pub called 'The Black Boy' where we could go at night to have a beer and a cheese sandwich with pickled onions. How we enjoyed those simple pleasures!

We marched and marched and our platoon was able to practice firing our mortars with blank bombs in to an empty field. We also practiced infantry attacks, and yet more bayonet fighting but were generally bored.

What sort of war was this? we asked ourselves. It was a very severe winter that year. On fatigues after meals we had to wash up metal plates in scummy water in the open. It was so cold that the metal plates froze together as soon as they were washed. One happy day we were piled into trucks and driven to the firing range at Colchester. There we were able to use live ammunition for the first time for both mortar and rifle fire which was very satisfying.

Meanwhile the 'Phoney War' in France had ended when the Germans launched their Blitzkrieg over France and caught our troops on the beaches of Dunkirk. It was then that the most famous rescue in the world took place. The Royal Navy and thousands of small craft managed, under heavy enemy gunfire and bombing, to rescue thousands of British and allied troops and bring them safely back to England.

While this was going on our Battalion had another secret move - this time to Wooler, a town in Northumberland. There we had to guard the beaches in case of enemy landings. We practiced all sorts of manoeuvres and keep fit

148

schemes and, you've guessed it, bayonet fighting. There wasn't a German in sight.

Eventually the great day arrived and we were issued with tropical kit and given embarkation leave. It was while on leave in Ilford that I met up with my friend, Gary, again. He was also on leave after coming home from Dunkirk with the remains of the Grenadier Guards. We met in the bar of the Super Cinema at the Ilford Broadway. Over a pint of beer or two, Gary told me lurid stories of his experience and made me feel a bit of a fraud - but my time was to come.

My embarkation leave came to an end all too suddenly and one of the last things I did was to visit Dad who was in hospital. When I kissed him goodbye, he had a tear in his eye and I had a sad feeling that I would never see him again.

Brownie Camp

By Jan Baldwin

"Goodbye Mum, goodbye Dad!" The end of weeks of anticipation - we were finally off to Brownie Camp!

What to take? What not to take? How much can I cram into my little suitcase (especially since mum had filled it with liberty bodices and fleecy knickers etc.)? Will I be warm enough? Will I get enough to eat? I'd better take plenty of Mars bars! etc. I was already about two stone overweight! I managed to get everything 'essential' in and my uniform was pressed and beret steamed. I was ready for the off!

I had no sleep the night before, of course, what with the excitement and nervousness. Was I going to go down with something that might prevent me from going? etc. But, despite the lack of sleep, the next morning at 6 o'clock we were all ready and waiting outside St James' Church for the coach to arrive.

Lots of tearful goodbyes were said, with most of the tears coming from the mums and dads rather than their offspring. Who would sit with who on the coach? Who would sit at the front versus the back? The anxiety continued and much had to be sorted out but, eventually, we were off. Isle of Wight here we come!!

My initial excitement as the coach sped along through the countryside gradually turned to boredom and apprehension as we got further and further from home and

Mum and Dad. When could we stop for the toilet? I never should have drunk that last drop of lemonade!

Everything worked out alright, however. We managed to find somewhere to stop and, after thirty little brown and yellow adventurers had made themselves more comfortable, we continued with our journey and eventually (after hours and hours) arrived at Yannouth in the Isle of Wight for our week of fun and adventure!

Camp was quickly set up when we arrived - obviously by the more experienced Girl Guides who were with us and the adult members of our party - while we concentrated on exploring the area and finding our bags.

The first night was okay. Everyone was so exhausted from travelling so we ate our regulation sausages and beans, cooked on the camp fire, before settling down in our allotted tents with our sleeping bags and groundsheets.

The next morning, after settling in and getting our bearings, we were off to Allum Bay cliffs to collect coloured sands. So it was back on the coach and off we went.

Most of that day is a bit of a blur as we were still quite tired from the long journey the day before and not too happy to be back on the coach. But we soon recovered and arrived at the cliffs, all armed with our little glass lighthouses that we had purchased to fill with our sands. We started to climb up the cliffs, digging out small amounts of pink, yellow and orange sand as we went and, before we knew it, were half way up a forty foot cliff. When, eventually, my little lighthouse was full (and after stopping to admire the fruits of my labour) I looked round and realised how far I had

climbed. I froze immediately and the next hour was spent
with Brown Owl and assistants trying to talk down a
slightly over-round Brownie from my precarious position at
twenty-five feet up! As I live to tell the tale, their efforts
were successful and (despite the fact that I held everyone up
and got told off for going so far) we made it back to camp
on time with me clutching my 'lighthouse' to my chest and
crying for my mum

That night the wind blew up and kept blowing out the
camp fire so 'tea' was a meagre affair of cold beans and
half-raw sausages. I really wanted my mum!

Then a storm broke out at about 9 o'clock that night.
There was both sheet and fork lightning plus thunder which,
on reflection, must have been a beautiful sight to see
(perched as we were on top of a cliff) but the general feeling
amongst the adults was one of nervousness and indecision.
Now, in my more mature years, I realise that the adults just
didn't know what to do to reassure us kids. The coach had
gone and there were no mobile phones in those days so,
eventually, we simply went to sleep amid the thunder and
lightning and howling winds.

Everything came to a grand finale at 3 o'clock in the
morning when I woke to find I was soaking wet and
freezing cold, and my two mates were sitting up crying. My
first thought was that I had had an 'accident' as little girls
are sometimes prone to do, but when I sat up I realised that
there was no tent! Flapping in the wind were the guy ropes
and a few belongings that were heavy enough to have
remained on the ground - the rest were flying out to sea to
join our tent! Thank God I still had my lighthouse! The

liberty bodices and fleecy knickers had joined the tent.
And that turned out to be 'it'. Those of us who had been
'de-tented' were shoved into the tents of those who hadn't
and, at the crack of dawn, the coach arrived to take us all
home - after only two days!

I have to say that I was never so happy in my life. I had
had enough of the outdoor life. My nose was running, my
throat sore and I just wanted to be fussed and cuddled.
All the way home I clutched my lighthouse (it was about
five inches tall and one inch round) to my chest. I wanted to
give it to mum and dad as soon as I got off the coach – and
to tell them the story of how I nearly died!

The coach pulled up outside the church. All the anxious
mums and dads were there, having heard escalated versions
of what had happened as each phone call was made and
exaggerated via the human 'internet' .

"Hello Mum! Hello Dad!" We all jumped up from our
seats and tussled with each other to be first off the coach
and the previous Saturday seemed like weeks ago.
We grabbed our depleted luggage from the driver as he
removed it from the hold and ran towards our mums and
dads, aunts and uncles, nans and granddads. Whole families
had arrived to collect the disaster-struck Brownie pack and
then, guess what, as I ran towards my family I dropped my
lighthouse!

Marie and John

By Marie Carr

Marie came back on duty at 5 pm. She had started work at 7 am but had three hours off during the afternoon and was now back until 8pm.

"The patient in the first bed on the right of the ward is going to theatre at 6pm – would you give him his pre-med please, nurse?" the sister said. Marie drew up the pre-med and went to the first bed on the right of the ward. "What's your name?" she asked. "John – what's yours?" the sailor replied. "Cheeky!" Marie thought, but went on to check his full details before giving him the injection. It would seem his ship was moored at the end of the pier and he'd had an appendicitis and needed an operation. He duly went to theatre at 6pm and Marie went off duty at 8pm.

The next morning she was back and, during the sailor's one week stay, she was very aware of his eyes following her around whenever she was on the ward. Marie had to admit that she quite liked this man but she wasn't the only one – some of the other nurses were very taken with him as well.

A few days after he had gone back to his ship, one of the other nurses appeared on the ward waving a letter from John addressed to Marie. "What does it say?" the nurse asked Marie. "How is he?" "Are you going to answer it?" "If not, I will!"

"Oh no you won't!" replied Marie and so followed several letters backwards and forwards from the sailor's ship to Marie's hospital and vice versa.

Eight weeks later 'John' came to Southend and met Marie's parents and, after that, he came as often as he could and soon they realised that this was something special. By the next Christmas they were engaged and, in the New Year, Marie went up to Newcastle and met John's parents and family and immediately felt she belonged.

Marie continued working at the hospital to complete her training and later qualified as an SRN. John in the meantime was still in the Navy and had applied to be part of the Field Guns Crew for Portsmouth. Many sailors were chosen but the training was really hard physically and there were several accidents but John was eventually selected to be part of the team and they were 'billeted' at Earls Court in London. A few times during that period Marie went to London to see their progress and also managed to see John actually taking part in The Royal Tournament several times. Once it was shown on TV and the lounge in the nurses home was packed with nurses eager to see their old patient.

The following year – Marie and John were married – just a quiet wedding but it's what they both wanted.

Marie continued working at the hospital but when she found out she was pregnant, she gave in her notice and moved down to be with John in Southampton. He was now stationed at a shore base – HMS Diligence at Hythe - and although he worked during the week they mostly had their weekends together.

John played football for the shore base against other teams in the Hampshire League and Marie was able to meet up with several other naval wives.

In July their son Jack was born and Marie's parents and family were able to visit. That Christmas, Marie, John and Jack then travelled to Newcastle so that Jack could meet his dad's family. By this point, the couple had decided that, since John had completed nine years in the Navy, it was time he became a civilian again. So, in January 1956, John, Marie and Jack went back to Southend and John set about finding work. They lived with Marie's parents for a month but then rented a flat in Hadleigh and John started working for Shell at Corringham.

They stayed in the flat for about a year but when Jack was almost killed by a falling ceiling it prompted them to start looking for a house of their own and they moved into their present home in May 1957. In February 1958 their daughter was born and their own little family was complete.

The years flew by and, in 1975, both children (now adults) left home. Jill started training as a nurse and Jack joined the forces but not the Navy – he chose the Army. He joined The Royal Military Police. He stayed there for over two years but was not very happy so jumped at the chance to transfer to the Army Air Corps and train as a helicopter pilot.

In the meantime, John had retired and, in 1982, he and Marie went on a trip round the world to celebrate. They were away for six months and visited Marie's sister in New Zealand and John's sister in Australia and promised themselves many more trips in the future.

Jill by now had qualified as a State Registered Nurse and went on to become a midwife as well. She and some other nurses had also gone to Australia – to a friend's wedding and had loved the country – so Marie and John were not really surprised when she told them she was going out there to work for a couple of years. She left in November 1987.

Jack had also finished his training and, as a helicopter pilot, was posted to Germany. He was married now with a family of his own – a girl and a boy – and Marie and John were able to spend several holidays out with them in Germany. Later Jack was posted back to England – to Middle Wallop in Hampshire. After this posting it was very easy for Marie, John and Jack to spend more time together and they often went to air shows around the country.

In 1989 there was an International Air Show at Middle Wallop (the Army Air Corps base) and at the end of the show there was this buzz of engine activity. Suddenly, sixty-four helicopters rose up from nowhere (or so it seemed) which was a fantastic sight and amongst them was the Army Air Corps Helicopter Display Team with one of the pilots being Jack.

Marie and John realised just how lucky they had been in life – especially with regard to their children. Jill had followed in Mum's footsteps and loved her nursing while Jack had followed dad and here he was – thirty-five years later - taking part in a military display. He was entertaining the public just as John had done at the Royal Tournament in 1954.

Yes, they had been extremely lucky and were very proud of their children. John and Marie felt that life had been very, very good to them.

The 'Old Girls' Return To St. Joseph's, Kalim Pong

By Ivor Cleverley

My name is Ivor Cleverley and my wife's name is Sylvia. I visited India in the late 1980s where Sylvia and other members of her family had been born. To summarise; her family were all born in a place called Shiliguri right up in the foot hills of the Himalayas. There was Cynthia, Lorna, Eva, Sylvia and William. Their father was in the army and had been stationed there. Bearing in mind there was very limited education and few facilities in Shiliguri, when they became old enough for school, the children were all dispatched (for the major part of the year) to a convent called St. Joseph's up in the hills near Darjeeling - a place called Kalim Pong. This convent had something like three or four hundred pupils, many of whom were the children of ex-patriots. Very few of these children belonged to the local ethnic population.

As part of our trip back in the 1980s (and Lorna and Dennis - Sylvia's sister and her husband - were with us) we did the usual run of various parts, moving east and finally finishing up in Shiliguri. We then went on to Darjeeling where we set ourselves up in the Windermere Hotel and planned a visit over the hill, over the river and up the other side to Kalim Pong.

The trip there was quite eventful; I arranged the hire of a Land Rover which managed precisely 200 yards before breaking down and, after acquiring another Land Rover, only managed to drive for two or three miles at a time before repeatedly having to fill up with water. Fortunately, we were able to draw water from the numerous Chora (waterfalls) that were coming down the hillside. Finally, we crossed the Teester River on, can you believe it, a Bailey bridge! This is a portable pre-fabricated truss bridge, designed for use by military engineering units to bridge up to 60 metre (or 200 feet) gaps and strong enough to carry tanks as they did in the Second World War.

After making our way over the bridge, we eventually found the convent of St. Joseph and knocked on the large imposing gate. We were greeted by a 'doorman' type person who then took us in to see the sister in charge of the establishment.

When we explained that both Lorna and Sylvia had previously been pupils (I prefer the term 'old girls'), the nun in question became very excited and said "God has sent you!" She continued, "Today is the day when we present all the prizes to the children for their work during the year and for the various examinations they have passed and I am going to ask you if you would kindly help us do the presentations by standing on the platform and handing out the prizes". Lorna, who is never slow in coming forward (unlike Sylvia) was very happy to take the leading role and I was relegated to the position of photographer which is no more than I deserve.

The entire operation went off without a hitch. We were then given a lovely meal in the refectory and taken round the convent which had changed quite considerably since 'the old girls' were there. We then had a trip to the chapel where I was finally able to realise a lifetime's ambition; I was able to use a toilet in a Nunnery Convent and leave the seat open and up!

We then embarked on our return journey; down the hill, back over the river and up the other side with numerous breakdowns. It was, by now, getting dark when we were confronted with what appeared to be motorcycles coming towards us. In fact, what we were seeing were Land Rovers coming the other way with only one headlight switched on. We discovered that drivers preferred to use just one headlight because it saved bulbs!

We finally arrived at Ghoom, which is a junction on the railway that goes up from the plains, and were invaded by a group of bodies commonly known out there as 'Gundas'. We considered them potential robbers and it took a bit of a fight getting them to remove themselves from the back of our Land Rover - they were desperately trying to get a free ride into the next town.

We finally arrived back at the hotel where Lorna's husband was waiting with bated breath. In all, the trip was a wonderful experience and neither Sylvia nor I will ever forget it.

About A Child

By Beryl Dore

His name is John – now a young man of almost thirteen, a very handsome young man, tall for his age, hair almost black and neatly cut and shaped by his mummy. He has the most beautiful blue eyes that seem to question your every move, your every word. He has a lovely clear skin and a smile to beat all smiles.

John was born on August 4th 1989 and he weighed 6lbs 4ozs: a beautiful baby and all seemed well. He'd been born by Caesarean Section but was a very contented baby and hardly ever cried. He just cooed happily in his cot or pram.

However, when John reached three months old, he suddenly went into a convulsion. The doctor was called immediately and, as he arrived, John had settled down and was sleeping peacefully. The doctor asked many questions and tried to reassure us that it was quite common for babies to have convulsions if their temperature rose but he wanted tests to be carried out and a series of appointments would follow.

Visits to Southend General Hospital commenced and then we found ourselves at Great Ormond Street Children's Hospital where John was given loving care and attention. John would still look at us as if he was really trying to study our innermost thoughts, as most children do, and yet there was something not quite right. We were not over-concerned but wanted to find out what the problem was and whether or not it was serious.

He was growing into a lovely little child. His weight and growth were coming along fine, he was eating and drinking normally and, gosh, how he loved his food! He was four months old now and had had his scan which sadly showed John had Epilepsy. Medication was prescribed and so John's little life went on quite happily – yes, he had his fits, but Mummy and Daddy learnt how to cope with them.

When John was approaching four years old, things were not right and tests were continuing. He was such a dear little fellow and his eyes would still follow everyone about but he was not talking and walked rather unsteadily. Having said this, John was thrilled to be up on his feet - a bit of a show off really - and why not!

John lived in his own little world, however, and did not ask questions. To this day, we are never sure what he is thinking.

The final diagnosis came when he was four years old. It was Cerebral Palsy along with Epilepsy and he was also double incontinent. This diagnosis was sheer torment and heartbreak for the family - especially mum, dad, sister Stacy and brother Tom who had the real sadness to bear. However, all of the family were remarkable. Throughout John's young life, he has had wonderful care and support from his close family and slowly but surely has grown into his own lovely person.

He now attends Glenwood School for Children with Special Needs in Benfleet, Essex. And with great love and patience from the wonderful staff there, John has been able to learn small things in his own way. He loves sport and will play for hours with his beloved darts on a special magnetic board. He also has his own small television and video set along with his favourite films to watch but, mostly, he loves to watch the World Darts Final and snooker. On these occasions, he sits in front of the screen in wonder. John never gets bored and loves ball games.

At school, they have a special theme every three months. It might be Gardening, Animals or Nursery Rhymes and John always goes dressed for the occasion (as do the other children). I remember him going dressed as a Doctor and he looked really great in his white coat, with a painted moustache, horn rimmed glasses and stethoscope! John doesn't really understand what these themed sessions are all about, but takes part with a wide grin on his face.

Today, at thirteen he is very tall, very handsome and a lovely lad. He spends a lot more time in his wheelchair as he becomes taller - his legs find it more and more difficult to carry his weight. He has a small vocabulary and, when you arrive to see him, he says "Whose that?" and greets you with the biggest smile.

John takes a lot of medication to keep his fits to the minimum, and the ambulance is called out frequently, but the paramedics (kindness itself) stay with him for a while and don't always have to take him to hospital.

John enjoys swimming with his mum in a special pool - most children with Special Needs find swimming very enjoyable and relaxing. We the family have come to the conclusion that, had John been born a normal child, he would have been a great sportsman with a fabulous personality. Clearly this wasn't to be but we are all very proud of him and award him a gold medal! We are quite sure that, in John's mind, he feels like a great sportsman and feels very happy. And yes, I expect you may have guessed by now that I am John's Grandma.

First Love

By Beryl Dore

She was a young girl of ten years old - and too young for true love – but, in the not too distant future, her fate awaited her.

She had been invited with her parents and her young sister to her auntie's wedding. Her auntie was marrying a young man by the name of Cyril and the ceremony was to be held at a nearby Registry Office. The young girl was really looking forward to the wedding and finally October 21st 1942 arrived. The Second World War was, by this time, at its height and the Registry Offices were very busy at this time - young couples were choosing to marry in the knowledge that their partners would be going off to war very soon and this is what was about to happen to Cyril.

The wedding went very well. The bride wore a dark costume with a pretty white lace blouse. She had a small jaunty little hat with matching accessories and wore a white Gardinia in her button-hole. The young girl thought her Auntie looked lovely standing next to her proud and smart Royal Marine husband. They looked like a very happy couple.

The young girl felt very grown up in her new dress and, with her hair neatly dressed in plaits, she looked very nice. After the wedding, the relatives and friends gathered outside to have photographs taken and, of course, to throw rice which was used in those days instead of confetti. What fun they had! The reception was held at the bridegroom's sister's house and, during the war, because food was on ration everyone helped with the buffet. It was a lovely spread and the wedding cake (a decorated sponge) took centre stage. Everyone was having a lovely time singing and dancing when, suddenly, the young girl glanced at the bridegroom and noticed another young man standing by him. This other man was also a Royal Marine and, thought the young girl, looked very handsome. "He must be Cyril's younger brother, Freddy, that I heard auntie speak of," she thought. The reception continued and later that evening, when everyone had said their 'goodbyes', the young girl's family made their way home. A good time had been had by all.

The war continued and, on March 3rd 1945, there was a family tragedy. The young girl's grandparents were killed by the last V2 rocket to fall on their town just before the end of the war. The grandparents were the parents of the young girl's father and her auntie who had married the Royal Marine. The family were devastated, just like so many other families living through the war.

But then suddenly, into the life of the young girl came Royal Marine Freddy once more (Cyril's brother). He was now twenty-three and she thirteen. He was on leave and hurried over to help the young girl's father and family salvage anything from the grandparents' home. He spent some time with the family drinking tea and talking about the tragedy while the young girl looked on. She had recently started to take notice of the opposite sex and, I suppose, had a school girl crush on the Royal Marine. However, sadly Freddy did not reciprocate except to be very friendly. Time went by and boyfriends came and went. It was now the summer of 1948 and the young girl was sixteen years old. She had become a young lady and was working as a clerk in the local Post Office. Then, returning from work one lovely summer evening, the young girl spotted two young men leaving the park. They both looked very handsome in their cricket whites and it was, of course, the Royal Marine Freddy and his younger brother Eric. They had a little old Morris car and offered the young girl a lift home. She accepted and her heart began beating like mad – just from sitting beside Freddy in the car! As the car approached the young girl's home, Freddy asked if she would care to write to him and, of course she agreed. They waved goodbye and she couldn't wait to get into the house to tell her parents the news. Sadly, however, the young girl's father was less enthusiastic. "Certainly not!" he said. "He is a man of the world and you are only a child of sixteen!" This broke the young girl's heart but she listened to her father as one did in those days.

And so life continued once again with teenage fun – dancing and parties. The years continued to slip away but the young girl often thought of Freddy and wondered where he was and if he had ever settled down with anyone.

The young lady's auntie and Cyril (Freddy's brother) whose wedding she had attended in 1942 had just had their third child, born on April 5th 1952. The young lady was visiting the family to see the new born baby - a little boy called Peter - and there, in the upstairs bedroom, was auntie looking radiant and Cyril the proud father. But then, wonder of wonders, Royal Marine Freddy was there too! By this time, the young lady was twenty years old and Freddy was twenty-nine so the age gap had closed. As the young girl's eyes met Freddy's eyes, they both knew that fate had at last stepped and they were falling madly in love. Neither had felt quite this way before and the young girl could feel strong vibes coming from Freddy. When he asked to walk her home, she felt she would burst! They chatted all the way home and, when they reached her front door, he mustered up enough courage to ask if she would like to go to the cinema with him that evening. You can probably guess what her answer was! The young girl's father now realised that his little girl was a grown woman and welcomed Freddy into their home. That evening in the cinema, Freddy lent across and took the young girl's hand - she was blown away with happiness and, after all these years, their romance was just beginning.

Freddy was serving in Germany and so the young girl and he only courted for six weeks. In between Freddy being abroad and being back on leave, the couple had completely fallen in love. It was now April 1952. In November 1952, the young girl and Freddy became engaged and were married on the 13th June 1953. They had a fairytale wedding with bridesmaids and spent their honeymoon in Hastings.

During the next five years, they had two children: Meryl and Robert and remained very much in love until, sadly, Freddy passed away on March 25th 2004. The young girl and Freddy had been married for fifty years. Meryl and Robert were married and presented the couple with five lovely grandchildren. The young girl's marriage to Freddy had been very happy, with just the usual 'ups and downs', but now that young lady has to get on with life as best she can.

You may have guessed by now that I, Beryl, am that young lady. I'm now seventy-three years old and dear Freddy was eighty-one when he left us. There is a large space in our hearts but we have some lovely memories.

He was my first and last true love.

Memories Caught

By John Gibbs

The first half of my life I lived on the Hertfordshire and Bedfordshire borders. I was born at the Benslow Nursing Home in June 1938 in Hitchin. Soon after the birth we went to live in Letchworth, still in Hertfordshire. The first few years there were spent living with one or the other set of grandparents. Unfortunately there was friction between my father and his stepmother, due to something that had happened before I was born.

Just before I was two years old, the Second World War began. As a result many things that had been available soon began to be in short supply. As a consequence, the Government issued ration books in an attempt to give everyone a fair share. Eventually, the Government decreed that all fit young men should be 'called up' to the armed forces in order to fight against the enemy. The only exceptions to the 'call up' were men employed in essential industries such as mining and farming. As a result, many industries became short staffed so the Government established a 'call up' system for young women to work in industries that had previously always employed men. Consequently, women began to work in skilled jobs in manufacturing and farming as well as the armed forces.

Before the Second World War started, my parents had enough money to make a deposit on a three bedroomed semi-detached house. However (when my father went overseas) my mother was advised by banks and building societies that, because property prices had fallen during the

First World War, it would not be sensible or possible to borrow money to purchase a house during the Second World War. This has been mentioned because property prices at the end of the Second World War were actually considerably higher than they were at the beginning. Consequently, my parents were not able (like many others) to use the services of a building society or bank during the Second World War and, therefore, were unable to purchase a property. Also, at this time (just before the end of the Second World War), there were very few council houses and most tenanted houses were owned by private companies. Many people were trying to find rented accommodation and long waiting lists emerged whenever a property was to become available. My parents were lucky to receive preferential treatment, however, as they had two young children. So we then moved into a three-bedroomed terraced house.

During the war, paper was in short supply – and this included toilet paper! So, like many other residents, we began to tear newspapers into small sheets and hang them on a nail in the toilet. However, newspapers were also limited to a few pages!

Electric light bulbs and electricity itself were also in short supply. The Government decreed that we should use low wattage bulbs. Most houses used twenty-five watt bulbs for the majority of rooms.

Toys were also very scarce and, one Christmas, my Grandad (being a cabinet maker) decided to make me a wooden pedal car. I had a marvellous time riding down the hill and then pushing the car back up the hill. On the following Boxing Day, my friend from around the corner asked to have a ride in the car but, after jumping in and speeding off, he lost control and crashed into a tree. The car was a write-off.

Due to the war and blockades, anything we used which came from overseas was in short supply. As a consequence, rationing was introduced for many items including clothing and petrol. Many food items, including meat and butter, were also in short supply.

In September 1943, I went to school. I had to walk two miles each way to and from school. We had to carry our gas masks. Every afternoon we went into the hall, took a mat from some piles, placed the mat on the floor, laid down and went to sleep. Writing this story, I have just realised that the sleep was an attempt to keep us awake during the rest of the day due to the interrupted nights from the bombing.

We were taught the '3 Rs' but I don't think the current generation at school would recognise them. Reading began with sentences like "The cat sat on the mat". Arithmetic consisted of learning, by rote, the tables from 1 x 1 = ? to 12 x 12 = ? Writing consisted almost entirely of being able to write the alphabet in Copper Plate. The children's toilets were outside and had no roof and no toilet paper. In the last year of junior school, my headmaster was R. J. Unstead who went on to be a noted writer of children's history books. After Junior school I went to a local Grammar school. In exams I was head of the class overall. At the end of the second year, the maths teacher marked my exam papers incorrectly. I told him about his error. Eventually, he checked my paper and reset the mark accordingly. At no time did he admit he had made a mistake. As a result of this incident, I lost interest in the school.

After the war ended, the items that had to be imported gradually began to arrive more frequently and in larger loads - and goods that had been in short supply became more common. After a while, the ration books discontinued. More exotic items then began to appear in shops - especially fruit and vegetables such as sweet potatoes, bananas and tomatoes which were almost unheard of prior to the war.

After I left school, I became a Police Cadet which was followed by two years National Service in the Royal Air Force. I then tried numerous jobs before becoming employed in the computing industry. I initially worked as an operator, then as a programmer and finally became an analyst. During this time, I met my future wife. We were married at the Registry Office in Luton, her home town, in 1966. Today couples can get married in many different places but when we married it was either Church or Registry Office.

Around this time someone introduced Green Shield Stamps into the UK. You were given some stamps when buying goods, which you then stuck in a book. After collecting a number of full books of stamps, they could be 'traded in' for goods shown in the Green Shield Stamp Catalogue. This craze lasted a few years.

After the end of the war, the volume of traffic on British roads increased rapidly – this was because many rail lines had been closed and an increasing amount of goods had to be transported. The Government of the day decided to build motorways to ease congestion and shorten travel times – the first motorway built was the M1.

In 1972 we came to Essex to live with our three children who were aged five, two and one. At this time it was rather difficult to buy a house. The problem was twofold. Firstly, house prices were rising at a very fast pace and, although there were now more potential properties to purchase, other people would come along and offer more money to buy a house already reserved by someone else. And then, by the time you had found another similar property, you'd find that the price had risen and you could no longer afford it. For example, we purchased a house in Luton for £6,000 and then sold it five months later for £8,400 but, before we had completed the sale, another person had offered us £10,000. Now, we chose not to let our first buyer down but, to make more money, other vendors did and this problem became widely known as 'gazumping'. The reason for our move from Luton was that I was offered a more challenging job as a computer analyst. I was given responsibility for a number of programmers and also had to ensure that a computer system was modified to meet the requirements of new legislation for the environment. Property prices later stabilised for a while but then began to increase rapidly again.

In the past, most people had lived close to where they worked but this was changing. I, in common with a lot of other people, was now living away from the town that I worked in.

Increasingly, new towns were being built near or around old towns and villages. This resulted in a number of problems. Firstly, when new towns were built they were populated from the run-down areas of large cities and, secondly, as more people began to commute the amount of traffic increased. The old town centres became almost derelict and in need of regeneration. Many new motorways were built and many town and village bypasses were developed. Because of this, we moved from Luton to Essex where we still live.

September 1939

By Joyce Hunter

It's September 1939 and the country has been plunged into war.

We children didn't think much about it at the time - I think we thought of it as a game to be enjoyed.

My brother Ron (eight) and myself (ten) were evacuated to Portland in Dorset. I remember getting on to the train and going on what seemed like a very long journey but I don't remember getting off the train.

Ron and I thought Portland was a very nice place to live - and so different from our home in Canning Town, London. The air was so much cleaner and fresher and there was lots of grass and fields and trees. We lived with a lovely family close to the town centre. They were very good to both Ron and I, and we were very happy there. However, because Dorset was a coastal county - with Portland itself being right on the coast – it was not a particularly good place to send us! We often went onto the cliffs to watch the planes – always military planes (I don't think private aircraft were allowed to fly over) and, I suppose, placed ourselves in danger.

One day we decided to go for a walk along the cliffs with some friends we had made from the town. We had heard that a German plane had crashed the night before and we all wanted to see if we could get a piece of the plane. Whenever a plane crashed, all the children in the area would want to try and get a piece to add to their 'collection'. Soldiers would always guard the crashed planes but would allow us children a piece.

We stuffed the pieces of plane into our pockets and walked away laughing and chatting - and pleased that we had managed to add to our collections. I was also pleased that I had managed to get a piece of a German plane for my brother Ron; he had not been allowed to come with us all on this particular day as he had to stay at home and darn his socks. Little did we know what was about to happen next...

As we were walking along the cliff by a big stone quarry (Portland is famous for its stone) and looking out to sea, we could see lots of aeroplanes circling around. As we watched on, the planes suddenly started to come inland. We stopped in our tracks and watched the planes thinking that they were British planes but then realised they had started to dive at us with machine guns blazing!

Some of us just dropped to the floor but others dropped over the side of the quarry. Fortunately, the drop into the quarry wasn't a steep one since we hadn't looked down before jumping over! We were all so scared. We all managed to escape with only minor injuries such as cuts and bruises - how none of us were hit by the bullets I will never know. I think that someone must have been watching over us that day and I often wonder whether Ron having to stay home and darn his socks was a good thing - who knows what might have happened if he'd been with me! It wasn't long after this that our mother (deciding that Portland was probably just as dangerous as being at home!) came and took us back to London.

Not long after we returned, the Blitz started and we were in the air raid shelters night after night. Bombs were dropping and machine guns were blasting all over the place and I was very frightened of the noisy German aeroplanes. The skies always seemed to be full of them and the noise would go on for hours and hours. When dawn came and the 'all clear' sounded, we would all come out of the shelters and look around to see what damage had been done - hoping that our own houses were still in one piece. Some places had direct hits and homes became piles of rubble with so many people killed.

It wasn't long after the Blitz began that Ron and I were again evacuated to a village in Huntingdon. But, this time, we were not able to stay together which was very sad for both of us.

This time the village was close to an R.A.F. airfield and every night we could hear the British planes taking off on their bombing raids. They would fly low over the tops of the houses. One night, one of the planes came down in a field quite near to where I was staying; it had been so overloaded with bombs that it wasn't able to take off properly. When the plane crashed, some of the bombs exploded and the force of the explosion broke windows all around the village.

Looking back, I am glad those days are gone. It all seems like a bad dream - a horrible nightmare – and one that I would never like to experience again.

I hope that, one day, in the not-too-distant future the world will be at peace instead of war. I hope that there will be no more suffering caused by tyrants who want to 'rule the world' and make other people's lives a misery.

Childhood Memories

By Hilda Miley

Now in my twilight years, I sit by my window and watch the children going home from school and think about my own childhood. Although I married, I never had children of my own but I watched and enjoyed my nieces and nephews growing up and watched them going on to have their own children and grand-children. I have sat and told them of times when I was a little girl and they have said, "Auntie, why don't you write it all down one day?" So now, with time on my hands, I will try.

I was born on the 28th October 1914 (that was two months after the start of World War One) at 12 Beaumont Road, Plaistow, London, E13. I was the youngest child of ten and we lived at the posh end of the road. I used to see other children who lived at the other end of the street running about in their bare feet and think, "How wonderful! I wish I could do that."

We were still quite poor - my father worked in the docks loading ships but it was only said to be 'casual labour' as there were not always ships in the dock. My mother was a lovely lady - very Victorian but very kind and always ready to help anyone who needed it. Poor we may have been but we were always warmly clothed and fed well. My mother was an expert at pastry-making and I remember coming in from school with the smell of her rabbit pie wafting through the passage - lovely.

183

As I said earlier, I was the youngest of ten children and my mother had already lost four babies before I was born. They died of either whooping cough or meningitis as there were not the cures we have today. Two died within two weeks and all this my dear sister Florrie told me in later life. I had a sister called Gladys who was two years older than me (I can just remember her) but sadly she died when she was six and I can recall going to her funeral. I can even still visualise the coat that I wore - it was small, black and white check with a black velvet collar.

I had a brother Lenny who was five years older than me and my sister Florrie, who I have already mentioned, was thirteen years older than me. I also had two brothers in their late teens and they both joined the Navy and served during the First World War. They were called Tom and Ted and I was bridesmaid to both of them when they married in their early twenties after the war.

I think my first memory was of the war - not that I knew much about it at that young age. I do remember a man coming round on a bike blowing a whistle and telling everyone to take cover - there were no siren warnings in those days - and mother would put Gladys, Lenny and I under the old-fashioned kitchen table until the raid was over.

I remember my mother kept chickens and we often had little chicks and even sometimes little ducks in the back yard. I also recall we had a big white cockerel; he was so proud and strutted around like the 'king of the castle'. I was always scared of him and, if I went into the yard to see the chicks, I kept well away from him. I used to like collecting the eggs from the nests and the neighbours would call at the house to buy them.

When I was very young, we had a little chapel next door to our house and on Mondays they had a 'Mother's Meeting'. My mother would make all the mothers their afternoon cup of tea which she would take through the little gate. A few years later, the little chapel closed down and was eventually taken over by a boiler-making firm. I used to go in there and watch the men working; there was a big fire in the centre of the building where they heated up the metal. The elder of the two partners who ran the firm was very kind to me and, at Easter time, would take me to the sweet shop to buy a big egg. One Christmas, the man brought me a big chocolate Father Christmas!

I was five when I started school, and very scared and shy of the teacher. I had only been going a little while when something bad happened; I wanted to go to the toilet but was too frightened to ask the teacher so I disgraced myself. We had an open coal fire in our little classroom, which had a tall fireguard around it, and the teacher hung my knickers out to dry on it while making me stand by them. I had to stand there while all the other children filed past to go out to play. I have never forgotten that dreadful day.

The school doctor and nurse visited school once a month to examine us and mother had to be there too. The nurse would also check our hair for lice. My brother Lenny and I went to the same church school - St. Andrews - and on Saints days after attending church we were given the rest of the day off. Sometimes on these days there would be a school outing and we would go to Loughton in the country by bus; there would be sports to play and later tea and cakes in a large corrugated building before going home. It was such fun.

Our school was a long building which was attached to the church and every Friday morning we had to attend church before going to classrooms. The infants had separate classrooms but the seniors had a long hall that was divided up by moveable screens. There were two screens for each class and they stayed there each morning only to be removed when school was over. It was the School Monitors' job to deal with these screens and, when I finally got to the senior part of the school, I always hoped that I could be a monitor but I never was. Another job for Monitors was to take round a tray of inkwells in the morning and place one on each desk and, sad to say, I never got this job either.

At one end of the road where we lived there was a little 'house-shop' as we called it because it was a front room converted into a shop. There would be jars of all kinds of things on the shelves. People didn't buy jars of jam as they do today - the jam would be in a large brown jar and you would take a cup and buy a few pennyworth. You could buy corned beef for two pennies and all sorts of pickles in a piece of greaseproof paper. There was a sweet factory at the other end of the road and the smell of sweets being made was wonderful. At lunch times, the girls would leave the factory and go to the little shop for corned beef and pickles for their lunch.

In the back yard of the same shop they sold coal. There was a pile of coal and huge scales with big separate weights for whatever quantity you wanted and two wheel trolleys would be standing by for you to borrow and carry the coal home on. Alternatively, a coalman would come round with his horse and cart laden with sacks of coal for direct home delivery. These sacks cost two shillings and tuppence and you knew you were buying the 'best nuts' as they called this coal. However, not many people in my area could afford this luxury. Only when my dad had a good run of work would mother buy a bag of coal from the coalman and he would carry it through the passage into our little kitchen before tipping it into the little cupboard. This was great because it meant that on cold nights in the winter we didn't have to go out into the yard for the coal. Sometimes, my brother and I would go to the 'shop yard' to buy fourteen pounds of coal for a few pence (this would happen when dad's work was short) but I thought this was wonderful because we had to bring it back on a trolley and sometimes I would beg my brother to let me have a go at pushing it.

There was another little corner shop nearby where you could buy a penny packet of tea; sugar was about two pennies a pound. The milkman came round with his horse and cart and, on the cart, he carried a large can of milk along with pint and half pint measures. A pint of milk would cost 1? pence and two pints would cost 2? pence.

There was also a 'Hokey Pokey Man' as we called him selling ice cream. He would cut the ice cream from a large oblong block and you could have a whole one for tuppence or a triangle shape for one penny. On Sunday, another man came round with real vanilla ice cream; he had two large silver barrels fixed to his barrow and one would contain lumpy ice cream and the other crushed ice with slices of lemon on it. My brother, being older, would say "Go and get me a tuppence of ice cream in a cup and you can have a pennyworth of ice!" The ice was quite pleasant really - especially if you could persuade the man to let you have a piece of lemon with it.

In the winter there would be the Muffin Man with a wooden tray on his head covered by a piece of rainproof cloth ringing his bell and calling out "Muffins!" Our family and neighbours would rush out to buy his muffins for tea and they were really scrumptious toasted by the fire and spread with margarine.

In the summer when it was hot and there had been a good crop of peas, a cart would come round loaded up with them. The pods would be all sweaty and nasty but the peas were all perfect inside and, of course, they were very cheap. There was also the water cart that came round to spray the roads when it was hot and dusty and the children would take off their shoes and socks and run behind it to get their feet and legs sprayed.

How I loved it when the Rag and Bone Man came! He would have cups hanging on hooks on his cart along with saucers and plates and other bits of china. If you gave him some old clothing, you could have a piece of china or a 'paper sunshade' as we called them. I really loved these 'umbrellas' and would beg mother to let me have something old to trade so that I could have one. The 'paper sunshades' were a piece of coloured tissue paper (for the umbrella fringe) stuck on to a piece of wood which became the handle. If I could get one of these it was wonderful - I would strut along like a real show-off.

Then there was the Salt and Vinegar Man. He would have a cart with a large barrel of vinegar and a great lump of salt and people would come out and buy what they wanted.

I also remember when I first saw men dressed up as ladies! They would come with a barrel organ and they would be wearing wigs, dresses and makeup. They would sing and dance while all the children would sit on the kerb watching. I don't think we actually realised that they were, in fact, men dressed up.

My friend Florrie who lived nearby and I would go to the local fish shop and buy ? pennyworth of 'cracklings' - these were skimmed off the oil that the fish had been fried in and were very crispy and lovely. We would sit on my door step and eat them until we were very nearly sick! In those days, you could buy a piece of fish for 1? pence and a really good piece of fish called Skate was four pence. If we were sent by our parents to buy fish and chips, there would be a real scramble. The youngest children would be pushed to the back of the 'queue' and had to keep shouting because they couldn't be seen over the counter.

I can't remember what year it was exactly - I must have been about seven - but a new young men's Christian Association (YMCA) had been built in the Green Gate

Street close to where we lived and King George V and
Queen Mary came to open it. All the children, myself
included, stood on the pavement waving our little Union
Jacks as they drove past in their horse drawn carriage. There
was a little cinema in the new building and, one afternoo,
my mother took me to the matinee. I don't remember the
film but I do remember the lady playing the piano and, in
the interval, we were served with a cup of tea and a biscuit.

We also had a little cinema called The Green Gate
(which I now understand is a bingo hall) and every Saturday
they would have children's programmes. I think it cost one
penny to go to the cinema as a child and there were several
long wooden benches in front of the screen. We would all
crowd on to these benches and, sometimes, the boys would
get rough and push us girls off the end. There were quite a
few actors – both funny and serious. We had, for instance,
Fatty Arbuckle, Charlie Chaplin, Harold Lloyd, Ben Turpin,
Chester Conklin, Larry Lammon, the Keystone Cops and
many more. The films were all silent of course - unlike
today, there were no 'talkies'. The programme would always
end up with a serial - usually the heroine tied up on the
railway with a train coming - so you had to go next week to
see what happened.

Also, on a Saturday in the summer, the men from the
local public house would have a 'beano'. This was usually a
day out to the seaside and, as they left on their journey in
'brakes' (coaches), all the local children would be there to
see them off shouting, "Throw out your mouldies!" In
response, the men would throw pennies out and all the
children would scramble for them while waving the brakes

off. Sometimes, on a Saturday afternoon, there would also be a man doing tricks outside the same public house. He could often be seen escaping, for example, from being chained up and tied up in a sack. If I had been sent on an errand to nearby shops at this time, I would join the crowd and enjoy the show.

I was naughty sometimes, like any normal child but I remember one particular occasion very well. I had to attend chapel every week on Sunday morning which was a halfpenny on the tram to get there so I'd been given one penny for my fare and one penny for the collection box. I had not been for two or three weeks, I suppose I had not been very well, but eventually I had to go again. I didn't really want to but my sister Florrie said I had to - she was really bossy and would often tell me off saying, "Because you are the baby of the family, you are spoilt!" So off I went to chapel. I got off the tram outside the chapel but, still not wanting to enter, I went to the nearby sweet shop and bought a pennyworth of sweets - you could get a lot for a penny in those days - and I stood there and ate them. I then waited for everyone to come out of the chapel and caught the tram home pretending I had been. The next week came and I knew I could not do the same thing again so I plucked up the courage and went to the service. Apparently, the week I missed they had set the children a competition and of course I wanted to tell all the family, including my brothers, about this competition. So when I got home I started to tell everyone my news, completely forgetting about the fact that I had not been to chapel the week before. Well, in my excitement, I must have been so jumbled up that my sister couldn't make head or tail of what I was talking about and she told me to shut up. For this, I became eternally grateful because I could have got into serious trouble. Although - as years went by - my sister and I became very close, I never ever confessed this secret to her.

I suppose it is true that being the youngest in the family can have its compensations and there were other occasions when my brothers and sister looked out for me. For example, when I went on outings with the school or chapel, I would leave my empty cocoa tin on the side (with a note saying where I was going and a drop-hole for coins) and my two elder brothers and my sister would drop money in it for me to spend.

My brother would tease me more than anyone else - he knew I was afraid of the dark and in those days there were no electric lights. We only had gas mantles at night and so you had to go upstairs in the dark. If mother asked me to go up to her bedroom to fetch something, I would grope my way up the stairs calling out loud "What do you want, mum?" knowing all the time what she wanted. As I then came back from the bedroom to the top of the stairs, Lenny would stand at the bottom calling "Here he comes! He'll get you!" and, to this day, I'll never know how I got back down the stairs. We did have some great times though. I can remember when we would sit on the kitchen doorstep and Lenny would try to catch the sparrows in the back yard. He made a frame with chicken wire and wood (it was made so that it wouldn't hurt the birds) and would prop it up on one side with a piece of wood to which was tied a piece of string and then we would sit and wait for the birds to go under for the crumbs he had left for them. When a bird went under,

Lenny would then pull the string and they would be in the frame. He would always let them go again like men who catch fish and then throw them back in to the water.

Lenny left school five years before me and became, just like a big brother, a bit demanding. His first job was in the city at a newspaper office and, one day, he came home with several annuals they had given him. They were lovely books and, if I asked him if I could borrow one, he would say "Well, ask me properly then!" and I would have to say "Please Leonard White of 12, Beaumont Road, Plaistow, E13 - may I borrow a book?" Sometimes he would then say 'yes' but at other times would say 'no' and the latter would make me really cross. He sometimes said "Go and get me some cigarettes, then!" but it cost two pence for five woodbines (in a green packet) and, if I said 'no', he would demand that mother make me go which always worked.

I remember once I tried to get my 'own back' - I kicked Lenny hard and then darted under the kitchen table out of his way. We had many laughs about all of this in later years but he didn't know until many years later that whenever he went out with his mates I would get his Meccano set out and, with two plates and eight wheels, make a pair of skates. I would tie them on to my feet and skate up and down the passage, which was really good fun. I always had to make sure that I put all the Meccano back before Lenny came home.

My eldest brother Tom used to tease me as well. He would say, "Cry and I'll give you a penny" and, after making me cry, he would say "Shut up and I will give you another penny". It was okay, though, because I'd finish up with two pence and I could buy a quarter pound of sweets for that.

When my dad came home from work, mother always had a hot meal ready for him and would always stand by the side of him and watch it slowly disappearing. He always left me a little bit - not because I was hungry but because dad's dinner was always yummy! It became a bit of a habit with me and made my older sister furious – she used to tell me off but I still continued to have my little taster.

Dad kept a little money box on the dresser - it must have been a war momento for it was in the shape of a tank with a 1914 soldier's head on it complete with a tin helmet - and now and again he would put six pence in it and if there was a good film on at the local cinema I would coax him to give me a six pence so that mother and I could go to the 'first house' to see it. Dad would go and line up in the queue while mother completed the washing at home. The cinema cost four pence for mum and two pence for me and mum would buy a two pence 'stick jaw' which was her favourite sweet. I would always be waiting anxiously for her to come but she always turned up just in time. I still had that little moneybox which dad called 'old bill' until very recently but have now passed it on to a younger member of the family to look after.

Having just had Christmas 2002, I'm reminded of mine as a child. I would hang up a nice clean pillow case at the end of my bed and wake up early on Christmas morning thrilled to find it full. We would be given an apple, an orange and a few nuts plus a couple of new pennies and a lovely white crispy new pinny which did up at the back and had pretty frills on the shoulders. When I think of the children today with their computers, televisions and mobile phones I am sure they cannot be as thrilled as I was. Christmas was a real family get-together. Mother would cook one of her big chickens and, with my sister to help, would stay up all night cooking Christmas pudding etc. Mother said that Christmas Pudding was not the real thing unless it was cooked on Christmas Eve. We would sit down to a lovely Christmas dinner and father would pour a little brandy on the pudding and set light to it - how everyone laughed and enjoyed themselves! After the meal, we would all go into our little parlour for a good old 'sing song'. Sadly, this all came to an end when our mother died. She was only fifty-eight years old and I was nearly fourteen. I had to grow up quickly then and, given my sister Florrie married soon after, life was never the same again.

I tried to keep house for Lenny and dad but it was never successful. There was some talk of dad re-marrying and I wanted to go out to work so I went to live with one of my older brothers and stayed with his family until 1941. At this point, I moved on to my sister's house and stayed there until I myself married.

When I reached my early forties, my husband died. But, although we had only been married for fifteen years, we had really happy times. So I found myself alone again but I wasn't really alone – I still had ten brothers and sisters!

I am now eight-eight years old and have many good wonderful times to look back on.

Foggy Memories

By Michael Robertson

I must have been about seven years of age. My father had returned from the war overseas and I was still getting to know him.

He returned to a very different London. He also returned to his original job - that of a glazier. He later became a sign-writer and glass embosser. In those days you could return to a job after a gap of six years.

My dad would work Saturdays - still part of the working hours of the week - and with war damage still prevalent his company had a lot of work especially in the Essex suburbs.

As there was no school on Saturday, I was allowed to go out to work with my dad. I would join the 'gang' and sit between my dad and the driver (who happened to live next door to us in Finsbury Park) in the van. We would start driving early and stop off after an hour at a café. This was the highlight of the day for me – a sausage sandwich with sauce and mustard and a large mug of tea. The day was long, and the weather often misty and cold, and a very tired and sleepy boy would often succumb to sleep in the warmth of the front cabin. I remember waking with a start on one occasion. I could not see anything through the van windows and could hear the gang in the back of the van shouting. The driver was leaning out of his side window and my dad had his passenger door open to allow him to stand and lean right out – there were no seat belts in those days!

Everyone was shouting "Follow the lights in front! It's the best we can do!" We were in a really thick fog or, as my Dad called it, a 'Pea Souper'. This was the second time I had seen a fog but it was still a shock. It left you disorientated, not knowing where you were. We had no compass bearings except the vehicle in front. Also, too much coal and fuel was being burnt and this had caused a yellow smog - it was hard to breathe. I was not frightened because my dad (whom I had only known for a year) sat beside me and the driver (who I called 'Uncle Ernie') was an ex-Army driver so I knew everything would be okay.

One hour later, and travelling at just ten miles per hour, we suddenly lost sight of the tail-lights on the vehicles in front. We had to stop. My dad got out of the van to see if he could guide us but called back to say "It's very muddy out here, Ernie, and the car we were following has gone down into the ditch!" In fact, it was worse than that. The area we had driven in to was very woody with many trees. We had landed in Epping Forest! We then discovered at least five cars in front of us – and that excluded the cars queuing behind.

It took all of us a long while to reverse out and get back on the road. However, thankfully a wind started to blow and we could see a little better. We arrived home but very late!

My dad loved to go to football matches as did all his brothers and, one day, I got to go with my dad too! Dad's oldest brother, Fred, had a car so off we went to Highbury - home of the Arsenal. There was not a lot of seating back then and we had to stand on the terraces - 38,000 supporters will just about fit in to the ground now but, back then, the number was closer to 50,000!

I asked my Dad if I could sit on his shoulders or on my uncle's shoulders but it was decided by all the 'flat caps' that I would sit with the St. John's Ambulance man at the front of the pitch near the goal. I was suddenly hoisted up, laid horizontal and carried over the heads to the front. When the game was over, I was returned the same way in reverse. I still don't know to this day how everyone knew where my dad stood in the crowd but find my dad, I did.

Many years later, I had my last incident with the fog (or smog!) in London because the Government of the day decided to ban coal-burning fires. (Smokeless fuel and central heating with gas were later to make an appearance.) My friend - a young Chinese man called Lloyd Thifen - had bought himself a three-wheeler (Messerschmitt) with a side-car and it was not long before he offered me a lift to work. We both worked for Standard Telephones. We had set off from Finsbury Park to Enfield along the Great Cambridge Road when the smog started to get thicker and, in no time at all, we were lost and facing a brick wall. We soon found out that we were in someone's garden. So, driving with the door open on the front of the side-car, we then had to follow the kerb. Whenever we got to a turning (and, therefore, lost our kerb), I would have to get out of the side-car and walk in front until we reached the next kerb. This is how it was until we finally got to work that day. We took the tube home as it was much safer!

War Years Memories

By Jean Moore

I was born in Crystal Palace in south-east London in 1932 and was the fourth child of six (three boys and three girls). One of my earliest memories was the tremendous crashing of glass and the red sky on the night that fire engulfed the Crystal Palace building. The huge glass structure, commissioned by Prince Albert and built in Hyde Park to house the Great Exhibition of 1851, had subsequently been dismantled and moved to Sydenham - not so very far away from where we lived.

My mother came from Cheriton, a small village near Folkestone in Kent, where she met my father who was a sergeant in the Royal Army Service Corps and was based nearby at Sandgate. By the time I was born my father had completed his army service and became what was known as a regular soldier on reserve. His civilian job was as a coach driver and I can remember many a happy trip to the seaside if there were any empty seats on his coach. Whether or not we went free I never knew, but I suspect we did!

In 1936 my father was re-called to assist in the transporting of the Duke of Windsor (who was Colonel-in-Chief of the Royal Army Service Corps) to exile in France following his abdication. I don't know how many drivers would have accompanied the Duke on this journey, but I remember being told that the driver had to be changed every ten miles. My father was involved in a similar exercise in 1939, just before the outbreak of World War II, to return the Duke to London. Of course, all this was top secret and very hush-hush, and as far as the inquisitive in the neighbourhood were concerned my father was simply away on his coach trips.

The family moved from Crystal Palace in 1936 to a flat in Hoe Street, Walthamstow – opposite the Baptist Church. It was compulsory for us to attend Sunday School and, as the church was so close to home, and we could be 'watched', there was absolutely no chance of getting out of it. In fact, we had to produce our text when we got home as proof of our attendance! After about a year we moved to a house in Forest Road, Walthamstow, where I attended Greenleaf Primary School and, later, McGuffie School.

I had a very happy childhood. My parents were strict and we knew how far we could go. My father only had to look over the top of his newspaper to restore order in the household! No arguments or tantrums – which is so often the case today. We made our own entertainment in those days. No televisions or computers to keep us occupied! We played on the streets - games such as marbles, hopscotch, knock-down-ginger. Oh, yes, we loved that one! We would tie one end of a very long piece of string to one door knocker and the other end to another door knocker, pull the string to knock on one door, run and hide in a bush or behind a wall and wait for the door to be opened. Of course, nobody was there! But when that door was opened the string would lift the knocker of the other door, which would 'knock' as the first door closed, and so it would continue until the string was discovered. A nuisance maybe, and I'm sure we were called some very choice names, but it was all innocent fun and we did nobody any harm.

We had a gypsy site nearby and all of us children played together. Their caravans were immaculate, both inside and out. Their glassware and china sparkled. Although most of the caravans were motorised by that time, some were still the horse-drawn variety and were beautifully decorated in the brightest of colours. I was always amazed at how much these people managed to store in such a small area. Everything had a place and everything was in its place. No room for clutter. They made wooden clothes pegs called 'dolly pegs' and would go from door to door selling them. These were so called as they looked like a little wooden doll with a round head and two 'legs' that would sit over the line and secure the washing.

During the war I was evacuated with other children from my school to Greenford in Bedfordshire. Every child carried a small case just big enough to hold a change of outer and underclothing, nightwear, slippers and toiletries, and a carrier bag containing a few basic items of food for the people with whom we were to stay. The remainder of our belongings were packed and transported separately. It was a very sad time leaving my mother and father, brothers and sisters, but I had my school friends with me and was very well cared for by a Mr & Mrs O'Connor, who had no children of their own.

I attended Harcourt School in Greenford, and the one thing that always stuck in my mind about that school was the yellow 'blackboard'! Yes – that's how I described it in my letters home – the yellow blackboard on which the teachers used blue chalk. I had never seen anything like this before and have never seen one since! I had good times there. Of course, there were fights between the locals and the evacuees, but that was all par for the course and we were all friends again after.

Unfortunately, during my evacuation I developed a mastoid (a painful swelling on the bone behind the ear) and was admitted to Bedford Hospital for surgery. Because there were no beds available in the children's wards I was put into a women's ward where some of the women had had similar operations. Sadly these women had ended up with paralysed and distorted faces which, for the seven year old onlooker, was extremely frightening as you can imagine. I decided that I didn't want to end up looking like that and did a runner! I don't know where I thought I was going, but I was quickly captured by the nursing staff and taken back. I finally had my operation, which was, in fact, carried out very successfully – not by the English surgeon who had performed the operations on those poor, unfortunate women – but by a German Jewish immigrant who had come to England long before the outbreak of the war and was a professor in this field of medicine. I considered myself very lucky indeed.

I left Bedford in early 1944 but couldn't return to Walthamstow as by that time we had been 'bombed out'. So we went to live with my 'Nanny Bickley' (my maternal grandmother) in Cheriton. I loved my Nanny Bickley. She was a lovely, cuddly nan and her house always smelled of newly baked bread and cakes. She did, however, have a very odd way of slicing bread! With one arm wrapped around the loaf and the bread knife in the other hand she would very quickly and skilfully saw off slice after slice – toward her rather than away from her – and I felt sure that sooner or later she would take off her bosom in the process!

My mother was a very good cook and, like all countrywomen, was able to make a meal from nothing and we never went hungry. A marrowbone and three-pen'orth of bones from the butcher always ensured a nourishing and tasty stew.

Not only was my mother a good and resourceful cook, she was also a professional laundress. Washing day was always Monday and doing the washing and ironing in those days was not quite the simple task it is today. It was shear drudgery! No washing machines, modern-day detergents, tumble dryers, electric irons in my young day, but wooden wash tubs or tin baths, rubbing boards, coppers for boiling the 'whites' and a 'dolly' (a wooden plunger for pummelling the washing in the copper), mangles with huge wooden rollers which would crush your fingers if you weren't quick enough to get them out of the way – especially if you were feeding the laundry through and someone else was turning the handle. Mangles were heavy, iron monstrosities and were usually kept out of doors which wasn't so bad in the summer, but on a freezing day with snow on the ground it wasn't much fun. And it was almost a competition between the neighbours as to who got their washing on the line first and whose whites (with the aid of 'Reckitt's Blue') were whiter than white!

Then came the ironing. For this my mother had an assortment of irons – flat irons of various sizes, collar irons, goffering irons (for frills and pleats) – which had to be heated by placing them on an 'iron' stand over a coal fire. Then to test if an iron was hot enough you licked a finger and quickly touched the sole of the iron and if it sizzled (the iron, not your finger – although it would if you kept it there for too long!) it was ready. If you weren't brave enough to do that, then you just spat on it! Ironing was an art in those days, certainly as far as judging the temperature was concerned, and it was all too easy to frizzle up that favourite, delicate garment by using an iron that was still that little bit too hot.

When my mother did finally acquire a washing machine she was not convinced that collars would come clean without some help, so it wasn't unusual to see her scrubbing away at these with a little brush first!

Like all families in those days the girls were always expected to be able to cook and launder and sew, whilst the boys would chop the wood, bring in the coal and clean the shoes. But my mother and father always encouraged the boys to cook as well and, indeed, my father was a pretty good cook himself.

We loved Monday's dinners. After the washing (which took virtually all day) there was little time, or energy, left to prepare a meal so it had to be something quick and easy. So Monday's dinner was always bubble and squeak, cold meat and pickles. For the uninitiated bubble and squeak was a fried mixture of leftover potatoes (roasted or boiled) and boiled cabbage and was best fried in dripping. But to get the 'real' flavour, it had to be ever-so-slightly 'burnt' so you had crispy bits! So on Sunday when we prepared the vegetables for dinner we had to do twice as many. "If you want to eat tomorrow," my mother would say, "you'll have to do more vegetables than that!"

Wherever we lived we were always lucky enough to have a bathroom. Not so at Nanny Bickley's. It was the copper in the kitchen (or scullery as it was known as then) or nothing. On bath night the fire was lit under the copper and in we got, one at a time, for our bath. I hated it. "I'm not getting in there any more!" I'd complain. "It burns my feet." But then along came the galvanised bath and from then on bath night was bliss. There was nothing nicer or cosier than having a bath in front of a blazing fire, finished off with biscuits and, that most comforting of all bedtime drinks, a nice cup of cocoa.

We stayed with Nanny Bickley until just before the end of the war when we moved back to Walthamstow.

And them came the street parties to celebrate peacetime. What a fantastic time that was! We were the only family in our street to own a piano so, with the aid of the decorators' boards, we heaved and pushed and pulled and thumped this weighty piece of furniture over the doorstep and out onto the street for the knees-up. Mr Howard, known as 'the piano man', did his bit for the celebrations. But it was Leslie Radley who could really knock out a good tune for the dancing and the singalongs. There wasn't much money around to pay for these parties and rationing was still very much in being, but we all pulled together and the Government provided funding, which was greatly appreciated. The community spirit was amazing. Everyone had a helping hand and a kind word for everyone else. Nobody had any more than the next person. Everybody was in the same boat and ready to rebuild their lives.

I was twelve when the war ended and so much had happened to me, as to everybody, in those few years. I'm seventy-three now and still enjoy life every bit as much as I did then and I have so many wonderful memories. There is still so much more to tell, but I think this will do for starters!

Memories Of Our Young Lives

By Grace Overall

I was born in 1911 - a completely different world to the one we live in today.

I lived in Clapton when I was very young and my parents shared a house with Mr and Mrs Cox and their daughter, Alice, who was just one year older than me and we remained good friends for most of our lives. I can remember the fun we used to have in the garden together – the Cox's lived upstairs while we lived downstairs. My father loved birds and he had a big aviary along the high fence which was full of birds of all species; small and beautifully coloured.

Margaret, my sister, was just twenty months younger than me. When she was born, she was very delicate, so she had to be nursed as much as possible with human warmth. Today, she would have been in an incubator. Fortunately she grew strong and healthy and lived well into her eighties.

Sadly the First World War was declared in 1914. My father was in a reserved occupation but, after losing brothers, felt he should volunteer to fight; he was killed in action in 1917. I remember it well; Aunt Margaret (his sister) and Uncle Harry came to the school and took me home to Mother. I was told I must not cry or it would upset mother further. I am ninety years of age now and can still remember it all like a picture.

Uncle Harry took us to see our first show, at the Stratford Empire when we were in our early teens, and we loved it! He also used to take us to London and we would walk round to St Paul's Cathedral, the Cenotaph, the Houses of Parliament and other places of interest. After he died, going through his letters we found one from our father from France asking Uncle Harry to see we were okay should he not come back from the war. Dad had also said that, should it go the other way, he would look after Aunt Margaret. Although, over the years, Uncle Harry became bitter and difficult I must say he did keep his word.

As you have no doubt seen in old pictures, children wore frocks or knickers below the knees but Mother always dressed us with them above the knees saying, "Children have lovely limbs so why cover them up?" We were lucky to have a lovely modern Mother. She went to work part-time (the war pension was very small) to give us a chance to belong to clubs (such as the Girl's Life Brigade and the Friendly Society) so that we could be equal with our friends but, even in those days, it all cost money.

We had hoops to bowl along, skipping ropes, tops to spin etc. And what fun we had! In those days, the side roads where we lived were almost clear of traffic apart from bicycles or horse and carts. Milk came on horse-drawn carts and, for many years, when the milkman came he measured the milk in a can and poured it into your own jug. Cream and cakes were delivered by the baker - weekly or daily if required - and of course there were plenty of corner shops that stocked all kinds of things. When very young I used to take a jam jar to the corner shop to get some jam out of a big tub.

Sundays we had to go to Sunday School and, in our day, we all wore hats and special Sunday Clothes. When we had grown out of these clothes (which were also used for special occasions) we used them for going out with Mother and were given new Sunday ones and so it went on. We also wore school uniform as children do today. Mother bought us some very nice hats for Sundays and, one Sunday, as we were off to Sunday School she said, "Now keep your hats on and don't allow other girls to try them on!" "Yes, Mother," we replied but of course we did! Later, we could not understand how Mother knew but when we came home we were met with trouble. "How did you know?" we asked. It turned out that Mother had been watching us from the back window - through a gap between the houses - oh dear! We never did that again.

Mother treated herself to a lovely crinoline hat for church on Sunday evenings but, of course, it had to rain and went out of shape! She carefully shaped it up, flattened the crown and put it on a vase to dry but my sister just could not resist putting her finger up the centre of the crown like a steeple and, when Mother saw it, was there trouble! It never dried in shape after that.

Margaret and I had what was known in our family as the 'Faulkner Giggle'. If anything amused us in a room full of company we would just catch a look at one another's eyes and we were off laughing to ourselves trying to control our giggles. Mother used to get so cross with us, but did admit she and her sisters were the same way. Most of the girls had it on her father's side of the family. As we got older, of course, we got better able to control our 'giggle'.

When we moved to a flat in Leyton, Mother took me around to the schools and allowed me to go to the school that I chose because it had a lovely circular garden full of flowers. I loved them when very young. The infants were mixed boys and girls, but the intermediate and seniors were all girls, separate. There were three floors; the ground floor for infants aged 5-7 years, the first floor for intermediate & senior girls aged 8-14 years and the top floor for intermediate and senior boys aged 8-14 years. Boys had a separate playground to us, and I can tell you some amusing tales about that!

On one particular day, on the way to school, the boys were playing around with us; taking off our school hats and running off into the boys' playground where we could not go. We ended up being late into school and got into trouble. We told our teacher the cause and she said "We had better go and get them then!" and, boy, were we scared! First we had to go to the boys' headmaster and then to the boys' classroom where the hats were handed back. We were left feeling very subdued but had had to tell on the boys to prevent ourselves from getting a severe punishing for being late!

Every year we had one week's holiday in Leigh-on-Sea. Mother used to save a small amount of money each week all year round to give us one week by the sea and in the country each year. Hadleigh (near Leigh-on-Sea) in those days was just a small country village and I can remember it well. In particular, I remember the Hadleigh Castle where we would play in and around the ruins. After we had had our daily dip in the sea, we would run back up the beach to

Mother who would be ready with a towel to dry us. We'd then quickly slip on some clothes and she'd say "Now run along to the nearest kiosk for ice cream or whatever and I will follow". Later, we realised that Mother wanted us to run so we were soon glowing with warmth. Even in those days weather was unpredictable, although more settled. We could leave our coats off for a month or more (except for the odd shower of rain) during the summer months.

When we were about seventeen (me) and nearly sixteen (Margaret), we had a holiday on the Isle of Wight and stayed in a 'Girls Friendly Society' holiday home. One night, however, we were late back and had to pull the bell (clank, clank) at which point every window opened and lots of heads popped out. When the matron finally opened the door, she sent us straight up to our bedroom although there was a twinkle in her eye so we were lucky. Coming home on the cruiser, we did not all have the 6d (old money) to stay on the top deck so some had to go below including Margaret and I. We felt badly about this as some of our church friends were on the top deck. It was all my fault as I had lent Margaret some money and forgotten I would need it back. We had to walk from Waterloo Station to Liverpool Street because we had no fare left to ride - and carrying all our luggage but laughing most of the way.

I remember the gas brackets we had for our light in the evening – they were fixed to the walls. We were in our later school years when, one day, we came home from school to find that the brackets had been removed and replaced with electric lights, similar to what we have today. Wonderful!

My First Memory Of The Second World War

By Doreen Petitt

My first memory of the Second World War was living in Barking, Essex with my family.

There were very few cars where we lived, so we could play in the street with no danger. Two children would hold a big rope across the road for us to skip. Some of the other games we played were Hop Scotch, British Bulldog and Marbles. We certainly spent much more time outdoors than the children of today. Some well-off families were just starting to get televisions. My older sister and her husband were the first people I knew to get a TV so, if we were on our best behaviour, they would let us watch it but it was only black and white back then.

We could walk from where we lived to the River Thames. A German plane must have flown along the Thames and got shot down. It crashed in the field at the back of where we lived. Lots of people - children and adults - all went to the plane to collect souvenirs. The boys liked to save bits of shrapnel.

During the war we had a gas mask in a case for use in a gas attack. We were not allowed to go anywhere without it but, fortunately, I never had to use mine.

There was rationing throughout the war and for several years after. We had a ration book, which you had to take to the butcher or grocer to get the very small amounts of food that you were allowed. Tea, sugar, butter, sweets and all meats were rationed.

Our main food was corned beef, which we had in many different ways. Potatoes and bread were also main foods because they filled us up. Even though there was a shortage of many types of food, I cannot ever remember feeling hungry.

We kept chickens and fed them on potato peelings and some sort of dried meal. They were kept for food and I can still remember them being plucked and the feathers going up my nose.

Everyone used to burn wood and coal on their fires but this contributed to the very thick fogs we used to experience, known as 'pea soupers'. One day we had to be led from school in a chain of children because we couldn't see our own hands in front of us!

Monday was 'wash day' and it went on all day. The boiler would be lit and we would come home from school and find all the windows steamed up. There would be a stew on the cooker while the washing was being done. My mum used a scrubbing board for cleaning the clothes and a mangle for getting the water out of the clothes.

We would have thick blackout curtains up at the windows and, if a warden came round and spotted any cracks of light, he would shout "Put that light out!"

My First Memory Of The Second World War

My oldest brother was in the Royal Air Force towards the end of the war. He used to fly over my school in his plane and wave his white hanky out of the cockpit so that I knew it was him; none of my friends believed me when I told them it was my brother.

I was one of eleven children and, being a big family, we had an indoor shelter made of steel. We learnt to play table tennis on it!

One day, on the way home from school, the air raid siren went off and a lady took us into her shelter.

Then, on another night, I remember a bomb dropping not far from where we lived. My sister pulled the bedclothes over us as the windows and doors fell in. My dad was on night work so didn't know what had happened. He came home to find broken glass everywhere and nobody in the house. I heard he was distraught and thought the worst, but thankfully none of us were seriously hurt and we had all gone to a relative's house up the road.

Lots of children were sent to live in rural areas in the war so that they were not in such danger from the bombs. My brother and I were both very young so my mother wouldn't let us be evacuated, but five of my brothers and sisters were. My remaining siblings were at work.

All those in my family who were evacuated went to Somerset and, to this day, have kept in touch with those they stayed with.

First Atlantic Crossing

By Dave Price

In May 1980 Jack called me on the phone to say he had a catamaran to take to the Caribbean and would I like to crew for him? Well, naturally, I jumped at the chance and a few days later I was helping to prepare the vessel for the voyage. It was one from the Canvey Island Boat Building Company owned by the Prout brothers who are well known for their catamarans. The catamaran we would be taking was a Quasar 50 called 'Concode'. Now this was my first 'cat' and it seemed enormous with a saloon the width of the boat and four double berth cabins. It also had a workshop with a bench, vice and tools. There was a Spronk head as the main toilet - that is a small compartment on the bridge deck with a hole that you sat on. You dropped your * * * * straight into the sea and the waves turned the 'toilet' in to a bidet! There was also a large gallery in one hull and a navigation area in the other hull.

Part of the preparation was finding two long, strong lengths of wood to make into spinnaker pose (why we did not have proper ones I don't know) for booming out the furling headsail and the stays for running with the trade winds hopefully. Another thing we did was to put thick Perspex over the ports in the hulls - Jack said the Atlantic waves were strong enough to cave the normal ones in! I think he was trying to scare us before we had even started. As seems usual with new boats, ours was not finished on time and we had to hang around for a couple of weeks before departure.

Besides Jack and myself there was a wiry beanpole named Jerry - an organic farmer from Norfolk - and Joe. Joe was a German and the boat owner's father; he had been the Brazilian Olympic Wind-Surfing team coach and, despite being about sixty years old, was very fit. Joe had been all over London trying to find a Panamanian ensign without any luck so he asked Doreen if she could make one which she did, very nicely and very quickly. Doreen also made us a lovely cake depicting the Atlantic Ocean with a tiny catamaran crossing it - it was so nice that it did not last very long once we started on.

Jeremy arrived with his kit the day before we were ready to leave and Joe arrived back late having fallen off the bicycle he had borrowed! He'd had to go to hospital to have eight stitches in a badly-cut arm. I removed these stitches a week later in the Bay of Biscay using a pair of plies and kitchen scissors!

We eventually departed from Tewkes Creek on the eastern end of Canvey Island at high water. It was 06.00 on the 22nd of May. We motored out to Southend pier head and from thereon we motor-sailed across the Thames estuary, round the North Foreland and coasted past Ramsgate and Dover using the new fangled auto-pilot. Just after passing Dungeness, the auto-pilot went off watch and we had to steer. Joe said that we needed to get it fixed, so Jack decided to go into Brighton Marina rather than go all the way back to Canvey Island.

Arriving in Brighton Marina in the early hours of the morning, we managed to get a bit of sleep before an agent came to repair the auto-pilot. He managed to make the repair successfully and we were on our way once again by the afternoon. For the first three days, it was all motoring into a south westerly wind until the wind veered to the west. At this stage, we were able to begin sailing and did so for the next two days. We sailed all the way into Bayona - a very pretty little harbour on the Rio Vigo which is on the Atlantic coast just north west of Spain and just a day's run south from Cap Finnersterre.

Bayona was a place I fell in love with. There you can find a hotel built into the ruins of an old castle and overlooking the estuary plus the Bayona la Real Yacht Club, also moulded into the old castle walls. We only stayed for a day, dining out at a fish restaurant in the evening and leaving the next morning after refuelling.

After having a good sail down to the Portuguese coast in westerly winds, we started to pick up the northerly trade winds which carried us all the way down to Grande Canaria. We arrived in Las Palmas five days later at 22.00. The next morning the fuel tanks were topped up and Jack said we should go down to Puerto Rico Marina on the south coast. We did do this and stayed there for three days. Joe was able to show us his skill on a wind-surfer after showing a local lad how to rig and sail it properly. It was very hot there, and you could not walk on the sands without shoes for fear of blistering your feet. It was now June 7th and we were leaving for the Atlantic crossing. However, one day out and the auto-pilot went on strike again. We all took a look at it and provided different views on what was wrong but none of us were right. So it was back on the helm for us. It wasn't too bad really and we soon got the feel of it. With the head and stay sails boomed out because we were running with the trades, Concorde almost sailed herself. We had seen several schools of dolphins already by this stage and it was always fascinating to watch their antics as they dived and rolled beneath the bows and leap right out of the waves just ahead of us.

Jack had been teaching me to use the sextant. It all seemed so easy because I was being told what to do and how to do it without having to get involved with the PZX Triangle that used to throw me when I was trying to work it all out from a book. My main problem was subtracting when I should have been adding and vice-versa, but I got the hang of it in the end.

Those of us who were not working on the cat would sometimes play cards (gin-rummy) which often determined who was going to do the washing up or get the next meal ready. It was mostly Jeremy who had to do the chores!

On a trip like this, you had to conserve water so there was no using the showers and washing with as little water as possible. I had some salt-water soap, that everyone borrowed, and bathed on the stern platform using sea-water. I had learned to look after myself as well as the vessel since there were no doctors or dentists out there.

It took seventeen days to reach Bridgetown Harbour in Barbados because we had been sailing in winds of force five give or take a few knots. A pigeon hitched a lift for a few days until it saw a large ship passing by and clearly thought it would be more comfortable and faster to take the other option! It took off as quick as it had arrived, and left Joe to clear up its mess! I was not terribly impressed with Bridgetown Harbour because it was too hot and there were lots of flies - the biting sort! I was glad to get the plane home five days later.

With all the experience I had gained on this trip, I was able to go to London Polytechnic School for Marine Navigation and sat the Ocean Yacht Masters Exam. I managed to pass and was given my certificate.

Anyone For Country Dancing?

By Alan Sharp

It was August 1959, I was sixteen years old and serving in a boy's regiment of the British Army, down in South Devon. I had joined the army a year previous, shortly after leaving school. Life was disciplined, sometimes arduous, always competitive and we all tended to make our own enjoyment.

Earlier in the summer a new commanding officer had taken charge of the regiment. He started to introduce and implement his own ideas on how he wanted the regiment to function. Some of his ideas were fine and completely acceptable, to most of us. But at least two were far too radical for a number of us budding RAMBOs to even consider.

1. He intended to form a Scottish Country Dancing Group
2. He wanted to form a 100 strong, male voice choir

Now at the time this worried a lot of us; there were mutterings about the place going soft! "It's turning into a bloody girl's school!" "Our street credibility will be destroyed!" etc.

One Monday a group of us were discussing, over breakfast, what we could do to prevent such a catastrophe.

"Let's have a protest!" said two mouthy Southerners (i.e. me and my mate Dave). "Great!" everyone responded. "What are you going to do?" We hadn't got a clue, but it was put up or shut up time and we were now committed to doing something.

Going back to our billet, we stashed away our eating irons. Then, improperly dressed without caps or jackets (which, in those days, the RSM could have you hung, drawn and quartered for), we both strolled out and through the wood at the rear of the barracks. We sat pondering what we should do. We were there by bravado and on impulse but it was almost 8 am and time for roll-call. We knew we'd be missed if we didn't turn up but decided to just keep on walking. We then decided to thumb lifts until we were either noticed or thought we had gone far enough with our protest.

At 2.30 pm, we wandered into Taunton Police Station and explained who we were. We were fed and watered and then locked up to await our escort back to the camp. On arrival back in camp, we were placed in the guardroom cells for the night. Next day, we had to appear before the C.O. to explain ourselves. We were 'in it up to our necks' as they say but we felt we 'might as well be hung for a sheep as a lamb'. We told the C.O. what we thought about things going a bit soft and he listened to what we had to say. After mulling it over, the C.O. then said "I am pleased with the initiative you have both shown in getting so far away under such circumstances. Well done! However, you were absent for 6 hours and 30 minutes – that's almost 7 hours – so each take 7 day's close arrest. March out!"

Anyone For Country Dancing?

For the next week, Dave and I both felt about six feet tall but only because our feet didn't touch the ground! Normal close arrest wasn't nice but, for us, the Provost Staff who ran the guardroom tried at least 50% harder to make life as difficult as possible.

From 6 am until 10 pm we belonged to them. They gave us both a 'real beasting' as it's known in the services. Fortunately, we were both very fit lads in those days and the physical effects on us were not to bad. The humiliation of being chased all day made us all the more determined to take what they were dishing out and not complain. On about the 5th day of our sentence, the C.O. paid us a visit and asked us how we felt. We said in all honesty that "It was hard but we could see it out to the 7th day." He then told us, before swiftly leaving, "Well done, keep it up!"

We completed our sentence and then returned to normal everyday routine. For a couple of weeks we both enjoyed a certain amount of celebrity within the regiment but nothing much, if anything, was changed by our protest!

As for the C.O., whenever our paths crossed, he would always make a point of speaking to us. It was only with hindsight that I understood what a real gentleman he was and how much he did to improve our lot within the regiment.

He did get the Scottish Dancers and he also got the 100 strong male voice choir and, guess what, both Dave and myself joined that choir!

Memories

By Alice Smith

Alice is a ninety-year-old lady who is bright, chatty and has a wonderfully clear mind for her age.

I met her through her son Colin and daughter-in-law who were kindly donating some craft materials to the centre where I work as a volunteer.

Colin told me a little about Alice which interested me because, like Alice, I also had a strong interest in craftwork. I asked if I could meet her.

Due to health problems, Alice had only recently settled into a local residential home so a colleague and I went along to visit. We were greeted with a lovely smile and a friendly chat and we soon got to know each other.

Alice was born in Melbourne, Australia to an English father and Australian mother. When she was seven years old her father decided he wanted to come back to England and so they all duly returned to the family farm in the Epping area.

After a while, her father purchased a piece of ground in Thundersley Common in Thundersley, Essex and built his family a home. Alice remembers, as a child, walking across the common to milk their cow; she would carry the bucket back home and be given a glass of milk for her reward. She thinks she was one of the first pupils to attend Dark Lane School and well remembers the local duck pond that was filled in many years ago.

At fourteen years old, Alice got her first job as a trainee milliner in Hamlet Court Road, Westcliff. In those days, flowers for the hats were not bought in - they were hand made by the milliners. Her creative knowledge and skill widened until, in the end, there was not a craft that she had not mastered and then taught!

Alice married in 1939 and had one son, Colin, who was frequently called into help prepare materials for the next classes his mother was due to teach. He did not enjoy this job because his mother was a perfectionist. When he reached driving age, he became his mother's means of transport from one venue to another (usually two venues a day) where Alice would teach her crafts.

Alice became one of the leading crafters in Essex, and was constantly being asked to do demonstrations at various locations and for many organisations including schools and colleges. If she could not make an appointment, a small group of her 'special pupils' would take her place. Alice was also called upon by Essex County Council when their own tutors were not available.

Between 1955 and 1964, Alice spent most of her time demonstrating and judging competitions for the Horticultural Society; she has many photos of the wonderful displays she judged.

Although Alice lived alone from 1978 after losing her husband she, until very recently, lived surrounded by her beautiful work and memories of a wonderful career.

Pathfinders

By June Smith

I slid into a seat at the back of the room as quietly as possible. I hated being late but the times of the meeting had been changed and I could do nothing to alter a previous arrangement. It was the second meeting of the Memory Catcher group and I had come along to learn how to be a 'buddy' to one of the people in the room. Everyone seemed to have stories to tell but I couldn't see I had anything to tell that would interest anyone. We passed around objects dating back over the last eighty to ninety years and chatted happily about the memories they conjured up. A pair of wooden butter pats immediately took me back sixty years...

I was then ten years old and the war seemed to be coming to an end. Due to my father's poor health he had stopped working in Fords foundry and the family helped to fund a small grocery business in Southend. Although my brother (who was seven) and I were very young, we were still expected to help with the business. When I got home from school I washed and put on an apron and had to cut large blocks of lard and margarine into small briquettes shaped with the 'patters' and wrapped in greaseproof - quite a feat when you think these large blocks weighed half a hundred weight to start. At that time the country was still suffering food rationing. Butter came in half-pound packs and these had to be cut into 2, 4 and 6oz amounts. Even at this young age it did not take long to cut accurately. When I think of my own grandchildren now, who are some years older than we were back then, I think they would struggle to get a presentable portion.

Things like sugar, rice and washing soda all came into the shop in huge sacks. We had to make paper cones out of greaseproof, brown paper (when available) and newspaper and then fill and weigh them to the allowance for each customer. I still, to this day, hate making paper cones; I vividly remember just how frequently the cones would fall apart and my shoes would always be full of rice etc.

In this day and age, young people are sometimes surprised that the packs of bacon in a supermarket come from a pig. In the mid-forties, bacon was delivered to our shop as a side of bacon. My father had trained as a butcher and it did not take him long to teach me how to bone the sides of bacon so that he only needed to chop the side into joints. I can imagine the faces of health and security officials at the thought of what we did, but fortunately I never came to any harm.

We did have leisure time as well and throughout the last sixty years my main hobby has been to sing in amateur groups. At that time in Southend we had a lady called Madam Freda Parry who was heavily involved in the Co-operative Choirs in the area.

They were adult choirs but Madam Parry was aware of a competition being held in London, open to young girls all over the country. Madam Parry scoured the area and, fortunately for me, came to the children's club that I belonged to called 'Pathfinders'.

There she found three young people (myself included), trained us and then took us to London to perform where we did very well. I remember that we performed in a very large building with lots of steps leading up to it and it had a huge stage. We all took it in turns to go on to the stage and sing. Once we had finished singing, we left the stage and went down some steps through a big fancy door. We stared in awe as we then caught sight of the tables which had been lined with food like a banquet – and for us! There was still a huge food shortage and we were now seeing lots of food we had never seen or even heard of (let alone eaten)! There were these magnificent trifles with what I can only describe as huge cream castles on the top!

Afterwards when we left, a photographer who was waiting outside took our photographs and, later on, when Madam Parry took us to the train station to meet our parents, we noticed an Evening News stand and there was our photograph on the front page! When we returned from the competition, the local press also carried the stories.

Because she knew my father would never allow me to have lessons, Madam Parry trained me for the next nine years in her own time and at her own expense. In return, I sang at lots of places for her including the Women's Institute and places like that. My strongest memory is from May 8th 1945. It was V.E. Day and I remember being taken across the road from the shop to the open area beside the White Horse Pub in Lifstan Way where there was a huge street party. I was to lead the singing and was perched high up on wooden crates looking down at this huge sea of faces with my father below me accompanying me on an accordion, while I sang all the old favourites; everyone joined in.

Madam Parry taught me that I had been given a great gift and it has always been used for pleasure, except when much younger when I entered competitions. I am sure neither of us would have thought I would still be singing sixty years later!

My Memories As A Child Of Eleven In 1939

By Betty Sommerville

It happened on September the third (a Sunday) in 1939 at eleven o'clock. I was with my mother, and we were in Kent as it was the hop-picking season. We heard a siren sounding, which told us that we were at war with Germany. As a child, I did not understand what 'war' actually meant. When the hopping season was over we went home. Our train pulled in at Woolwich, Arsenal. We had a bus to get, and waiting at the bus stop, we heard guns being fired. I was afraid and when we reached home we could see that the docks were alight. I shall never forget that, ever.

My sister Eileen and myself went to stay with friends who had a cottage at a place called Hartest in Suffolk. It was way out in the country and there was no transport where we were. So if and when we had to do shopping, we had a very long way to go. I think it was a good mile to walk.

One day my sister and our friend and me decided to go to the few little shops they had in the village. As we were walking along, coming towards us were two men, and they stopped and asked us the way to Hartest. We were told later that these men were German soldiers and they had been picked up by our boys and arrested.

On our return from the village, as we were walking along, an aircraft was overhead and was flying quite low. We heard a machine gun starting to fire and realised that it was us they were firing at! So we dashed for a ditch and hoped and prayed that all would be well. Obviously, I am here to tell the tale so we were lucky!

My sister and I decided that perhaps we should go home to be with our parents and the rest of our family. We had two brothers (one was in the Army and the other in the Navy), three more sisters living at home and two sisters who lived away from home – one was married and one had volunteered for the Land Army.

My Mother went to work at the Becton Gas Works whilst the war was still on. We were having air raids with 'doodlebugs' and rockets and never knew when they were going to hit.

When I was fourteen I was old enough to go to work. I would have just about reached home each day when the siren would go off so we mainly had our evening meal on our laps in the air raid shelter until the 'all clear' sounded. Some nights, when a raid was particularly bad, we would be in the shelter all night long with dawn prompting the 'all clear'. On one occasion, the bombing had been particularly bad and we were soon contacted with some very bad news; my brother-in-law, his brother, two sisters and his parents had all been killed with a direct hit on their house - they had not stood a chance. My sister (married to the brother-in-law) had been evacuated with their two children to Wales. It was like a nightmare and one which I will never forget.

My Memeories As A Child Of Eleven In 1939

My sister Gwen was already in the Land Army, and at that time I was not old enough to enrol. So when I reached seventeen, I went to Writtle and signed on to become a member of the Land Army too.

My first post was somewhere outside of Colchester - a place called Boxtead - well out into the countryside. As I recall, on the first day we were taken by lorry to a farm quite a distance away and asked to pick potatoes. It was back-aching work but, finally, we returned to our billet. Unfortunately a few of the land girls (including me) took exception to the person in charge. We had returned to our room one day to find that the beds we had made were stripped. We were then told to remake them again and this continued for some time. As a result of this, some of us put in to go to another place; happily we were posted to Royden in Essex.

It was a big house and had lots of rooms so I shared the bedroom with eight other Land Army girls, which was so nice. In fact, one of the girls named Beryl came from the same town as I did. We had a very nice matron who really took care of us. We used to have our breakfast around about six o'clock and be on the lorry by seven to be taken to the farm.

The country folk were all very nice to us Land Army girls. When the Land Army finished I still kept friends with some of the girls, but do feel sorry that two of them have since died. This was one of the best times of my life.

So many things happened in the war years and I do thank God that most of my family survived. Unfortunately some people did not make it. We were all issued with ration books, which we used for some time even after the war ended. As a child I did not have chocolate and, when my daughter was born, we were given a ration book for National Dried Milk.

It was great when, at last, we won the war. Everyone had a glorious time celebrating and going back to leading their lives.

The day I met my husband was on a Saturday night. At the time I was a supervisor at Woolworth and one of the girls was talking about going to a dinner and dance at the Ruskin Arms that evening. She invited me to go too - I could be her guest because she was a member of the 'Winkle Club'.

I was introduced to some other friends and didn't, at the time, know that one of them would become my husband! His name was Jim and he was so easy to talk too. He had the way of someone you have met before. As for me, it helped to have a boyfriend like Jim because until I get to know someone, I don't always know what to say to them.

The next week Jim asked me out to see a film. The cinema was in Manor Park and that was our first date. After that, we saw each other quite a lot. From meeting him in January 1950, we got engaged in August and were married on March 24th 1951.

238

My Memeories As A Child Of Eleven In 1939

We had a double wedding as my sister Eileen and her future husband Ernie decided to get married as well. We had a lovely time but I can't say much about the weather - it rained, it sleeted, it snowed and the sun shone. You name it, we had it! But it was still a lovely day.

In 1953 we had our daughter and this was the happiest year. When she was born, she became 'the apple of our eye'.

I am grateful that I have been able to put pen to paper in order to recall these memories and hope that there will never be another war where so many young men and women lose their lives.

King George V And Queen Mary's Silver Jubilee, 1935

By Fred Spence

At a scout's meeting in April 1935 we were informed that a group of scouts were required to attend the parade on the historic day in May – King George V and Queen Mary's Silver Jubilee. To be fair, all the scouts' names were put in a hat and the scoutmaster picked out the required number of names to attend the function. I was one of the lucky ones. I was seventeen at the time.

On the day in question my parents called me at 4.30 a.m. to get up and wash and put my uniform on.

Following breakfast I left home and went to the meeting point which was Mile End Underground Station at 5.30 a.m. where I reported to the scoutmaster in charge of the party.

Also waiting at the station were a squad of police officers. When the station opened we proceeded to the platform which was for London bound trains. When the train arrived, it was quite full of passengers going to London.

We got off the train at Charing Cross Station, as did most of the other passengers. As we came out of the station, there were crowds of people milling around and making their way along the route to find a good viewing point.

Our group of scouts had to make our way to Constitution Hill and report to a depot.

At the depot we were told we would be selling programmes. I was told I would be selling my programmes to the people in the stands.

I was given some programmes, a numbered badge and collecting box. Programmes were priced at one shilling and two shillings and sixpence.

I was taken to a stand in Constitution Hill. I had to position myself, with the programmes, at the top of the stand as that was where the people would be entering the stand after producing their official tickets.

When the procession started I was to remain at the back of the stand so I would not obscure people's vision. It was a lovely day and everybody was in good spirit. When the parade was due to pass we could hear a band playing in the distance and people cheering. Being on the stand, I had a good view of the parade. Towards the end of the procession came an open landau with the King and Queen in. They acknowledged the crowds with a wave of the hand and a bow of the head. The crowd was in a happy mood and pleased with the day's event. People in the stands clapped and some stood up when the Royalty went by.

After the parade had passed we had to report back to the depot and hand in our programmes, collection box and badge. The scout group kept in one spot and we had our lunch there. Following lunch we made our way back to Charing Cross Station to catch a train back to Mile End Station. At Mile End we dispersed and went home. When I arrived home the street party was going on, so I changed and joined in. The following morning I received a letter from St. James' Palace thanking me for my services.

No Regrets

By Joan Stevens

My story spans over forty years but I have decided to begin in the year 1955 – June 1955 to be precise. I have chosen this time because it was one month before my 18th birthday and it was when I considered that I was leaving my childhood behind and entering the 'adult world'.

I lived at home with my parents and my brother who was eight years of age. We lived in Dagenham, Essex but because our house was on the border of Dagenham and Barking, my senior school was in Barking.

On leaving school, I trained as a telephonist at Seven Kings Telephone Exchange and in 1955 was working as a telephonist at the Bank of England. During the week I would travel to London by train and, most mornings, usually met several of my friends (those who also worked in the city) on the platform. As soon as we got on the train, we would talk non-stop until we reached our various destinations. Sometimes we would meet up again during our lunch hour and we would either go to the 'West End' to shop or sometimes to the Fleet Street Jazz Club.

In common with most teenagers of my age, my greatest passion was shopping and this would either be for records (which were 78 inch and made of vinyl) or buying clothes and make up. My favourite artist was Frank Sinatra but I also collected records by other artists including Nat King Cole, Ella Fitzgerald, Frankie Lane and Johnnie Ray. I remember my mother taking me on two coach outings with her firm to the London Palladium to see Frankie Lane and Johnnie Ray and, on both occasions, all the teenagers screamed like mad when the artists came on stage. The only exception to this screaming was the instant hush when Johnnie Ray began to cry singing his famous record called 'Cry'.

I loved buying all the latest fashions; the favourite item of clothing that I possessed at the time was a brown gabardine pencil skirt and waistcoat and the skirt had a detachable flying panel. Other clothes that I liked wearing were dirndl skirts that had to be worn with a very starched petticoat and a wide elastic belt around the waist. Shoes were also a passion of mine. The fashion at the time was platform soled shoes and the more tiers to the platform, the better my friends and I liked it. Another fashion fad was berets; my friends and I all possessed a beret and we would wear these flat on our head, with a very large hatpin through the top. My friends and I all owned a long thin umbrella and we would take our umbrella out wherever we went, whether or not it was raining. The handbags that we carried were called 'envelope bags' because they were the shape of a long thin envelope. When I think back to how we must have looked to our parents, it is not so different from the young people trying to make their own fashion statement today.

During the week, my friends and I would usually meet up in the evenings at a coffee bar at Blakes Corner in Barking. We would sometimes stay there for several hours drinking 'frothy coffee' and discussing anything from the latest boyfriends to pop records or what we would be wearing on Saturday to go dancing in.

Saturday was always my favourite day of the week. During the day I would go out with my friends and we would either go shopping or perhaps just look at things we intended to buy with our next wage packet. By teatime, we would make our way home to wash our hair and have a nice long soak in the bath ready for the big Saturday night out. Our most frequent haunts were the Bath's Hall at Barking, the Winter Gardens at East Ham or the Ilford Palais. The music we danced to was, I think, far more interesting than what the young people of today dance to. Most of the clubs and discos today invariably have no live music and the sounds are all set up by a D.J. I consider we were fortunate, as the music we danced to was always provided by live bands. The bands would alternate around all the different dance halls. Bands that appeared at our venues were: The Ted Heath Band, Jack Parnell, Johnnie Dankworth (before his marriage to Cleo Lane) and The Ray Ellington Quartet. We would also see Lisa Rosa and Dickie Valentine who were the singers that appeared with the Ted Heath Band. The popular dance was the 'jive' and the faster you were able to twist and turn the better. For the very slow dances, we did the 'creep'. We always hoped to have the last slow dance with the boy that we fancied just in case he asked to see us home.

Sundays during the summer months were usually spent at a large open-air swimming pool in Barking Park. My friends and I would cover ourselves in a mixture of olive oil and vinegar and bask in the sun until we were bright red! We must have been completely mad, but no-one talked about skin cancer in those days. We would be in and out of the water swimming and playing ball and then when we were dry we would eat our packed lunch and return home in the evening happy and exhausted. On my Sunday outings to the swimming pool I would often take my brother Brian with me. Brian was nine years younger than me, but he loved swimming and all my friends encouraged me to bring him along as he was such a great kid and never presented any problems - he just enjoyed himself playing ball and swimming with us.

Until Brian was born I had been an only child and I hated this fact and longed for a brother or sister. The reason that I was an only child was because I was born in 1937 and prior to my birth my father had been a soldier in the regular army. At the outbreak of World War Two, he was immediately called up and he spent the majority of the 'war years' overseas so my parents thought it was not the time to bring another child into the world. Brian was born one year after my father was demobilised. This was a dream come true for me and I loved him from the moment I first set eyes on him. I helped my mother feed him, bathe him and dress him. I was also allowed to take him out for a walk in his new bouncy pram. I enjoyed watching him grow into a cheeky toddler, getting into all kinds of mischief and cried with my mother when he began his first day at school. I would always try and watch him play football on a Saturday morning and I would cheer like mad when he scored a goal.

Brian was with me at the swimming pool on the Sunday that I first met Roy. As usual I was with my friends and Roy was with a group of his friends that we had seen around and admired from afar. The boys were about four years older than us and big and beefy as they were very much into weight training. Needless to say we all fancied them like mad. Terry who was our age and one of our crowd was Roy's cousin and he introduced me to Roy and soon the two groups got together. My friends and I were in 'seventh heaven' and could hardly believe that we were mixing with the 'big lads'. Although Roy was initially very shy, he did invite me on a date to the pictures with him the following week. After our first date we began going out together on a regular basis. After a short while we met each other's parents and discovered that our fathers knew each other from their school days - they had both attended the Westbury School in Barking - so when the two families eventually got together they had plenty to talk about.

Roy and I became engaged one year after our first meeting and planned our wedding for August 19th 1957. We had a lovely traditional white wedding. I had three bridesmaids in dresses of lemon and lavender. June who was Roy's sister was my chief bridesmaid and my two cousins were the other two. We were married at St. Margaret's Church in Barking and held our wedding reception at the Municipal Hall in Barking. My parents paid for the reception and wedding buffet and Roy's parents paid for the evening buffet. One hundred members of our family and friends enjoyed the day with us - a day that I will remember for the rest of my life.

The following morning we set off by coach to spend two weeks honeymoon in a small hotel at Broadstairs in Kent. We were young, happy and excited - both wondering what the future held for us - as we embarked on a journey of married life together.

An Autobiographical Account

By Doris Stone

One of my earliest memories is of being taken with my parents on a shopping spree to London. It was nearly Christmas, all the shops were aglow with bright lights and tinsel and all the people seemed to be carrying large parcels with very cheerful happy faces.

On the way home, there were the most peculiar noises coming from a brown paper parcel held by my father. This, later on, turned out to be a large china doll which was saying 'mama' and 'papa'. The fact that this doll had already had its neck broken and repaired mattered not one bit to me; we were not very affluent at the time.

Several years after this, father decided we were too old for such things and we were introduced to books and music instead. My big brother and I would meet at midday and go to lunchtime concerts at the National Gallery, then of course there were proms which I attended regularly when I lived nearer to London. It mattered not that I came home alone on the train at midnight with a ten minute walk at the end – I felt safe and was not afraid. I don't think this can be the case now.

At around this time I worked for the Ministry of Labour and, on one occasion, had to go before a Judge up north to swear that I had issued an enlistment paper to a certain Frank Jenkins - a deserter. Incidentally, his mother came to do my mother's washing which made this request of me even more uncomfortable.

I used to go to several London concert halls and listened to Madame Butterfly and La Boheme. But after this came the real stuff; Beethoven, Bach, Mozart, Chopin and Tchaikovsky with a little Scott Joplin thrown in for light relief.

I have always been a lover of classical music - this runs in the family - and there was always good music in the house which helps to explain my musical side. As for the words, I have always been an avid reader and read almost anything excluding Ruby M. Ayers and Barbara Cartland.

I married a chap in the Royal Navy at the young age of twenty-three and we had a wonderful five years, However, he died when his ship was torpedoed. I then re-married to someone in the R.A.F. but I'm not too sure that I cared much for the man and made him promise that he would let me go if things did not work out. Needless to say, we carried on quite happily and produced two children; Phillipa and Nicholas and our marriage lasted 30 years. My husband died at the age of fifty-eight.

My daughter Phillipa, then working at Lloyds Bank, became very restless. Her two best friends had moved away - one becoming an air hostess and the other going to Clare

College, Cambridge - so she decided to go to France as an au-pair. I admired her for staying the course, because the family were so... fussy. They not only wanted the tea towels arranged symmetrically but insisted on having the soles of there slippers polished! While in France, Phillipa met up with a very nice man called Jean. He had a dear little son who was about five and eventually married Phillipa who went on to produce two daughters and a son.

The Life And Times Of Sally Young

(an excerpt from her full autobiography)

By Sally Young

My Father's name was Alfred and his brothers and sisters included Tom, Joe, George, Walter, Arthur, Amy, Alfred and Jane - there were others but I didn't know them.

My Mother's name was Lillian (her maiden name was Williams) and her brothers and sisters were William, Percy and Florence.

I was born on the 20th November 1913 and my first memory was when, as a three-year-old, my Aunt Amy was washing my grandmother [her mother, who was very sick - I think dying] and she asked me to fetch the soap. I'll never forget the overwhelming feeling of self-importance I felt when I handed it to her.

During World War One, we lived at 81, Mortimer Road, Kensal Rise, London. I remember how excited I was when we all dashed under the stairs and sat on the coals during air raids. I was too young to be scared but my brother Will always had an upset stomach – I'll always remember the combined smell of coal dust and diarrhoea.

On one occasion, a bomb landed right outside our house and created a large hole in which I played with my little friend Frankie Mann - two years my junior. (More about her later.) When the hole was filled in, I cried. Then, one cold November day, the sky was grey and everyone was looking upward. I saw what looked like a long grey sausage overhead. There was a shout of "Zeppelin!" and I was snatched up by a tall man and had to duck while he chased into the house and under the stairs in the dark. I found it all very thrilling.

The first war ended when I was nearly five years old. I can remember dad taking us by bus to the other side of London to a large house belonging to his brother Joe and, here, I met numerous members of his family. I met Lillian (who was the eldest of his children, a war widow and much older than my dad who was her uncle) plus (and I can only remember a few names) a number of the others - Harry, Maud, Ivy and Grace. These young ladies were quite beautiful and made a great fuss of me. I felt rather important. Joe, who worked for Gilbeys, was like a huge beer barrel because he was so big and round. Every body was dancing and singing to some very loud music. I was bewildered - it was like a mad house with lots of drinking and waving of flags as they celebrated the armistice in great style. This kept on all night. The street was full of lights and crowded with noisy people, fireworks and balloons. When things became too hectic, dad took us into a back room and stayed with us. He did not drink very much and I do believe that he was probably the only sober man there.

There was a similar party a few years later when Maud married a member of Gilbeys and they were transferred to Australia which, in those days, was the end of the earth.

I did not meet any of these relations again with the exception of Jane - the youngest -whose name cropped up many times. She was arrested a few times for doing such things as riding her bicycle on the pavement. On one occasion, she was asked to stop and get off her bicycle but she chose to carry on and the police had to chase her. The worst thing about this for Jane was that she was wearing these longs called 'bloomers'! 'Bloomers' were introduced to England, I seem to remember, by an American lady - Mrs. Bloomer. On another occasion, Jane had the audacity to enter the high and mighty exclusive Men's Club. Terrible! No ladies had set foot in there before and it was recounted in the newspapers. She was arrested for this too. She was a rebel (and a disgrace to the Salisbury clan) but I can remember my dad having a good laugh and I secretly admired her.

When I was four years old I dearly wanted a scooter and one day there was great excitement and fuss. Believing that my dream had come true, I was sure I was being led upstairs to discover the scooter but, instead, I was taken to a tiny cot which contained a new baby boy - I wasn't impressed - all I wanted was a scooter! Later I was to appreciate (more than I can tell) the little lad who was to become my constant companion and joy for many years. He was my little brother Len.

After the First World War things were very hard - meat, sugar etc. were scarce. My dad bought baby rabbits and fed them up to help feed us and his sister - my Aunt Amy - who lived down the road. I was too young to realise that the baby rabbits would eventually be eaten by us and made pets of them. I was devastated when I found that I was eating Rosie and that May was due to be on the dinner plate soon.

I was always very close to my grandfather and considered myself to be his very favourite grandchild. He would take me into his garden and show me his new acquisitions - a toad named Tommy, a snake named Sam and fish in his huge bath. He also had four large figureheads from his Grandfather's and Great Uncle's ships - these were named Elizabeth, Mary, Jane and Martha and we would greet them every morning. They were painted in bright colours and I wish I had them now.

The Life And Times Of Sally Young

One day when I went to visit him - he lived at 1, Caroline Street in Camden Town (now changed to Carol Street), I saw a barrel of live eels outside a fishmonger's shop. I had heard that these were cooked alive. I watched them for a while and then decided that I would save some of them from that terrible fate. I don't know how I managed it but I took a number out and folded them into the skirt of my long dress. I scuttled away to my grandma's place and rang the bell praying that my granddad would answer and not my grandma. The former did open the door and took me straight along the long passage to his big bath of fishes.

This house was very tall and narrow and the staircase was almost vertical. There wasn't a bathroom - one had to wash in a cupboard in the kitchen and always with carbolic soap.

My first memories of gran's house were of numerous pictures of Lord Kitchener's very fierce-looking face; they were over the fireplace, on all the walls and even along the staircase. Even we kids had little discs with this same image pinned on to our jackets. He was gran's hero. He was the one who was saving our poor soldiers from being killed or even being eaten alive by the savages called Boers who were cannibals. I don't know where she got this information.

It became the fashion for men to put glue on their moustaches and twist the ends into sharp points. When kissed by them one's cheeks would invariably be badly scratched and bleeding. This fashion was not popular with the wives who very soon put a stop to it. For some reason I blamed Lord Kitchener for this fashion and his image as a hero began to fade as far as I was concerned.

As I became older and could read and reason things out for myself my ideas changed. I learnt that a 'Boer' was a farmer and not a cannibal and that my gran had rather the wrong idea about the Boer War but simply believed all she had been told.

My own grandpa was more of a hero to me than Lord Kitchener. My uncles (his sons) told me that when they were young they accompanied their father (he was an inventor mainly but also kept a plumber's shop) to the usual meetings on the street corners every Saturday from where he would always return home with a gold or silver watch and a black eye. In those days, the street corner cons stood on soapboxes and drew a crowd. Then they challenged men in the crowd to get out of different contraptions like cages or to get free of chains etc. If they succeeded they won the watch but otherwise they had to pay. Of course these cons never meant to part with their watch. However, my granddad would take his own inventions and challenge them back - he had the local crowd behind him so the cons had to agree. Invariably grandad won but the cons never had any intention of parting with their watch and it always ended with a fight for all. Grandad often ended up coming home with both the watch and a black eye. Grandma would give him hell when he arrived home so he would bribe her by giving her the watch.

A neighbour was asked to take me to join the infant's class but I refused to go there at first because I thought that an infant was an insect and I told them I wasn't an infant - I was a little girl. Although I spent all that time at Beethoven Street Infants School I never knew who Beethoven was - I thought he was the street cleaner with whom I had become very friendly.

When I was about five years old I was sent to a music teacher to learn to play the piano. To practice, I had to go to our front room which faced North and was very cold. We only used it for parties and, at those times, had a big fire. So for one hour I had to stay in there where no-one could hear me - no-one was really interested anyway. Then, because my fingers would be icy cold, I would warm them up by playing 'thunder and lightening' (rather than scales) up and down the piano. Boom! Boom! I would also bang the keys, imagining that people were running up and down the full length of the piano or that a football match was being played with the high notes playing against the low notes.

Eventually the long-suffering music teacher came to see my mum and said I never practiced and that she was wasting her money. I was in deep trouble. In years to come I was very sorry that I did not learn to play the piano.

Will, my older brother, and I were left by ourselves one morning and found a picture book featuring Dr. Squiggles who was bald accept for a few strands of hair on the top of his head. We started to fight as to which of us should be Dr. Squiggles. That afternoon we were due to go to a party and mum had put my hair into rags. These were strips of material cut into pieces about one and a half inches wide and ten inches long. There were no such things as rollers in those days. My hair was rolled into these. Will said he had the shorter hair and he, therefore, must be the Dr. Anyway, eventually we found a pair of scissors and I tried to cut his hair but my fingers were too small and I made little or no impression on his head. However, he then cut at all my curlers but managed to only cut about half way through each curl so all the rags looked intact. When my mum started to undo my rags, half the hair came away with each rag. I looked like a half-plucked chicken. She was terribly upset and cross and punished me rather severely. Finally, dad took me to a hairdresser who had to cut my hair short. I returned home feeling very happy - I smelt like a rose garden and knew there would be no more painful combing sessions and no more horrible rags! I dreaded what my grandma's reaction would be as she considered it wicked for a girl to have short hair. I don't remember seeing my gran for a time after this.

Most Sundays we would gather round the piano in Grandma's front room upstairs and have a singsong. Then everyone had to give a solo. Little Gladys always hated this and reluctantly recited "Twankle twankle leetel star" (she was supposed to be a French girl singing in English) before scuttling off. If grandmamma wasn't watching, I would join Grandad hiding in the dark corner behind the massive rocking chair and we would play roulette with farthings and halfpennies. More often than not, there would then be a shout from Grandma - "Jack, where are you?" - and a hand would appear, grab me and drag me back to the front room. Invariably, granddad would have a 'dressing down' – "You should be ashamed of yourself - betting on a Sunday and teaching the child to be worse than she already is!" This did not deter us, however - as soon as she was back fussing around and busy with other things, we would creep back to our corner again and continue our criminal activities.

The Corridors of Power

By Doug Powell

" I've fixed up a private visit to the White House and the Capitol" announced Maurice.

My wife Mary and I, on our first visit to America, were staying with Maurice some forty miles north of Washington. A few years older than me, he was editor of his local newspaper before retirement, so he knew everybody and everybody knew him. One of his acquaintances was Ros Bartlett, a senior Congressman, which made him the equivalent of a British Cabinet Minister. It was Ros who had set up the visit but as he was called out of town on urgent business his wife Ellen became our escort.

Mornings begin earlier in America than in Britain. Many offices, shops and schools are underway by 8 am. Our visit was timed for 8.30 whereas public tours of the White House begin at 10 am and queues start forming hours beforehand. Oh, what a lovely, lovely moment it was when our car glided along Pennsylvania Avenue and stopped to one side of the White House. Here we got out, strolling casually past those people who had been waiting Heaven knows how long. They must have wondered who on earth we were.

The next moment was glorious as well. Standing in the doorway were three members of the Secret Service (that's the Presidential security staff). Ellen said, "I am Ellen Bartlett."

They appeared only mildly interested and so she added, "My husband is Ros Bartlett". And what a dynamic reaction. "Yes, MA'AM ! Good morning, MA'AM! This way, MA'AM !" We were ushered in and Ellen mentioned in passing that Mary and I were guests from England which made us feel like royalty. It was the same for the rest of the day. Ellen merely had to announce herself as Ros Bartlett's wife and doors opened everywhere.

In the reception room we were invited to sign the Visitors Book. Mary suggested I sign for both of us but I wouldn't agree. "No, you do it yourself and then you can tell everyone that your signature is in the White House Visitors Book!" So there they were; our two names for future generations to admire. 'Doug Powell, Southend-on-Sea, England' and on the next line 'Mary Powell, Southend-on-Sea, England'. I wonder if our Queen and Prince Philip will one day pay another visit to the President and, as they have previously, sign that book. If she did and casually glanced back over a few pages she might say, "Oh Philip, look! Doug and Mary were here the other day!"

Private visitors see parts of the White House not included in the public tours and are escorted by a Secret Service officer acting as guide. The general public get no such help and are allowed just twenty minutes to see certain designated rooms upstairs on what is called the State Floor. And they don't get to sign the Visitors Book either. We were shown various rooms on the ground floor which were set out in exhibition style. One was the China Room. Presidents have always received government funds with which to purchase state china and we saw beautiful examples on display in a number of cabinets. But, as the years have passed, some items became cracked during use or slightly damaged and usually these were auctioned or sold off with the proceeds going towards the cost of new china. However, in 1901, Theodore Roosevelt's wife strongly opposed this practice. She insisted that any damaged china be broken up and scattered in the nearby Potomac River.

Upstairs on the State Floor we walked along the wide, impressive main hallway which is known as the Cross Hall and is covered with gorgeous deep-pile red and gold carpet. It leads into the large East Room, lavishly decorated in gold and white. This is the best-known part of the building, seen regularly around the world on TV news programmes. They set up microphones in that room when Presidents make announcement too. When Mary and I watch those items now we smile smugly. "We walked along that lovely red carpet. And look! George Bush is standing exactly where we stood!" Because it is so large, this room has been the scene of Presidential receptions and the weddings of three Presidents' daughters. It is also where Richard Nixon made his speech resigning the Presidency in 1974 after the Watergate scandal.

Then on to the Green Room which used to have a special feature. Thomas Jefferson, the third President, used it as a dining room and had a revolving door fitted. This door had trays on one side so that staff could place food on these trays and then revolve the door. Thus those inside the room could obtain their food in privacy without being interrupted. Quite unique, but it was scrapped when the room was refurbished in 1971.

One other room I'll mention is the State Dining Room because of the inscription by John Adams carved into the mantel - 'I pray Heaven to bestow the best of blessings on this house and on all that shall hereafter inhabit it. May none but honest and wise men ever rule under this roof.' Very noble sentiments but I couldn't help feeling that they are a little ironic, remembering that several Presidents have been involved in scandals; either political, financial or moral.

All too quickly, our ninety minutes were over and it was back to the car for the short drive to the Capitol. From this point on, we were exclusively Ellen's personal guests and I soon realised that the Bartlett name carried considerable influence. Here again the public have only very limited access to parts of the building but Ellen took us all over the place - she was in her element.

The House of Representatives had, the previous afternoon, been debating an amendment to the Annual Budget. Their decision had been taken to the President in the evening and so today they were to meet to sort out the details of the transfer. But the President had refused to sign the authorisation. In America, unlike Britain, the Head of State has the power of veto. So as it was, there was nothing for the House to discuss today and thus no session.

At the door leading into the Chamber, Ellen told the Secret Service men who she was and in we went. She had a great sense of fun and kept reminding everyone about 1814 when British marines set fire to the White House. "This is Doug and Mary, my guests from England. They burnt down the White House, you know!" In the Chamber, we sat in

266

the front seats while she explained the layout and procedures of the House. It was a fantastic privilege to be there - like sitting on the front benches of our own House of Commons. Looking up, I saw two groups of tourists in the public gallery gazing down at us. Huh, hoi-polloi, I thought!

The Rotunda in the very heart of the building is quite awe-inspiring. A circular hall, 96 feet wide, capped by that massive dome 180 feet high. All round the hall, immediately beneath the dome, is a frieze depicting historical events from Christopher Columbus through to the Wright brothers' flight at Kitty Hawk. On the circular walls are eight immense oil paintings. Ellen pointed to one showing the presentation of the Declaration of Independence with all the signatories gathered around. She indicated one man towards the edge of the group. "That was my husband's great-great-great-great uncle!" No wonder there was a note of pride in her voice.

Although the public see inside the Rotunda they cannot do what we did next. Thanks to Ellen, we stepped outside onto the balcony high above the street from where we had a wonderful view across the city; we could see Pennsylvania Avenue, The Mall and the breathtaking Washington Memorial - the world's tallest masonry tower. A few weeks before our visit it had been shrouded in tarpaulins as it received a thorough cleaning but was now sparkling white on this bright sunny day. I felt very honoured, knowing that few people were allowed to stand on this balcony. This was emphasised by a burly Secret Service officer closing the double door very firmly behind us when we moved back into the building.

As lunchtime beckoned we made our way to the staff restaurant where Mary and I encountered a small problem. We saw on the menu 'grilled ham and cheese sandwiches' and so I asked for "a grilled ham and cheese sandwich twice, please". I didn't realise that Americans don't know the word 'twice'. This caused a delay and I was told later that I should have asked for "a grilled ham and cheese sandwich two times, please." Then, at the cash desk, the lady was captivated by Mary's English accent and insisted on starting a conversation. I felt embarrassed because a queue was waiting behind us and so I tried to keep things moving by asking how much we owed for our lunches. All that happened was that she gazed at me open-mouthed and gasped, "Ah gee, he tocks like thett as whale!"

After lunch we went to the Senate Chamber - the equivalent of our House of Lords. They were in session and so we sat in the public gallery for a while. Only a handful of Senators were present and the one speaking was paying tribute to a prominent citizen from his area who had recently died. To me, without wishing to be in any way disrespectful, the most interesting aspect of the Senate was that this was where Bill Clinton had stood and faced impeachment over the Monica Lewinsky episode.

Senators and Congressmen have their own offices located in buildings across the road from the Capitol and a private underground railway provides a shuttle service. Ellen took us to her husband's office where the walls were covered with certificates, awards and diplomas. He is obviously a highly talented man who works hard for the people he represents and thus earns their respect and gratitude. The most memorable certificate was the Jefferson Award for services to America's space programme. I was disappointed that we didn't have the chance to meet him.

Ellen must have shown us almost every corridor and painting in the building. Everywhere she was treated with deference while we two guests from England were greeted warmly. We passed one door just as it opened and a man came out. "Good afternoon," he said. "Good afternoon," I replied and we each continued on our way. Ellen asked if I had recognised him - he was Dick Cheney. Good Heavens! The Vice-President himself! There are 276 million people in the States and he is 'Number Two' in the whole nation. That makes him one of the most powerful men in the western world and I had spoken personally to him without realising who he was. But there are two sides to the coin, aren't there? He hadn't realised who I was either! If he ever finds out he may boast to his friends, "One day I spoke to Doug from England. He burnt down the White House, you know."

Finally it was time to end our visit and to try to leave the city centre before the evening rush hour. But first let me set the record straight about the White House. Originally it was known as the Presidential Mansion. During the Napoleonic War, America was neutral and traded with both sides - Britain and France. This upset the British who then declared war on America. One night in August 1814 some British marines sailed up river, landed at Washington and under cover of darkness set fire to the Mansion. The inside was gutted but then a heavy rainstorm started. The force of the rain extinguished the flames, thus saving the outside of the building. As part of the repair work the outer walls were all painted white in order to conceal the marks of the fire. Thus it got the nickname of the White House and after a while this became accepted as the official name.

But I think I managed to convince people that I was not around at the time.

Wartime Memories Of A Gordon Highlander

By Malcolm McCallum

My name is Malcolm McCallum. When the war started on September 3rd 1939 I was nineteen years old and, having left school in Scotland, was living at home with my parents in Buenos Aires and working in an office job. I was having a very pleasant life but, along with very many Anglo-Argentines born of British parents in Argentina, I registered at the British Consulate volunteering to join the British Armed Forces when required. At that time there were only nineteen British Royal Marines to defend the Falkland Islands and so two hundred Anglo Argentines, with dual nationality (including myself), volunteered to go there. Without arms or training I wonder what good our presence there could have done! Anyway, I then fell ill with an appendicitis and so missed the opportunity of going there. At that time Britain did not want volunteers from abroad to join up, as ammunition and food were in short supply. My parents were requested to bring back my three younger brothers who were still at school in Scotland much to their annoyance. This was at the time when children in Britain were being sent into the country or abroad for their safety.

The South Atlantic was a dangerous theatre of war with the German pocket battleship Graf Spee and submarines, known as U-boats, sinking many of our supply ships. On December 13th 1939 the Graf Spee was spotted and engaged in battle near the estuary of the River Plate by the much lighter armed allied squadron formed by the British cruiser HMS Exeter and British and New Zealand light cruisers Ajax and Achilles, under the command of Commodore Henry Harwood. In a valiant battle, during which the allied ships suffered heavy casualties and damage, they managed to damage the Graf Spee to the extent that it sought refuge in the port of Montevideo, capital of Uruguay, across the wide River Plate estuary from Buenos Aires, and compelled her to seek sanctuary in Montevideo harbour to carry out repairs.

This encounter between the German battleship with much longer-range guns and the smaller allied ships became known as the Battle of the River Plate and resulted in much damage and loss of life on both sides. The Uruguayan neutral authorities ordered the German ship to leave within 48 hours, but the British consul, seeking more time for reinforcements to arrive, invoked an international law. This prevented an enemy war ship from leaving port within 24 hours of a merchant ship, and so arranged for ships to leave port at intervals! The British secret service through the press did a marvellous job spreading rumours that powerful naval units were on their way to engage the Graf Spee as soon as she left neutral waters. One was led to believe that many war ships were already there, when in fact the nearest ships were thousands of miles away! The Exeter in particular was badly damaged in the battle, but managed to limp down towards the Falkland Islands. There was great excitement as to what would happen next and all those who could, got into tall buildings in Montevideo to watch the ship move out. Captain Hans Langsdorff, a humanitarian and anti-Nazi, decided to scuttle the ship and ignore Hitler's order to go out and fight because he wanted to save the lives of his crew. He took them to Buenos Aires and there committed suicide on the German Imperial flag.

The Germans overran Belgium and France in 1940 and the British army returned home through the epic of Dunkirk. After that disaster Britain required to rearm her forces and did not want any more mouths to feed. It was not until 1941 that the British Consulate in Buenos Aires accepted volunteers to register for service provided they had a British Passport, passed a medical check-up, were nineteen years of age and had complied with their Argentine civic obligations.

In March 1941 my brother, Kenneth, and I set sail with forty other volunteers, twelve previously ship-wrecked crew and eight wool classifiers from Patagonia on the 'Highland Chieftain' - a transatlantic liner. She was armed only with an anti-submarine and an anti-aircraft gun and a machine gun on the bridge. She was fast enough to travel without escort through the U-boat infested seas. We took a zigzag course to avoid submarines lining up to fire their torpedoes on to our broadside, which works because submarines are slow to manoeuvre into position. By this time the German pocket battleship 'Bismark' had replaced the Graf Spee in the Atlantic. After leaving Montevideo, we crossed the South and North Atlantic following a huge 'S' course, going first towards the Cape Verde Islands off the African coast and then towards Greenland approaching Britain from the North.

273

The voyage took the whole month of March 1941. During the last stretch we saw a wonderful display of the northern lights, which were like thousands of searchlights in the sky of all shades of white, yellow, blue and green criss-crossing each other with the movement of the clouds. We took turns doing submarine watch, looking for the tell-tale feathered wakes made by their periscopes. We did one hour on and one hour off duty in a four-hour watch before having twelve hours rest before the next watch. On quiet days we were able to play deck games, swim and partake in any other activity on offer.

In very rough weather we were strapped in our posts for fear of being washed overboard. Nevertheless it was most unlikely that any submarine would attempt to surface in such conditions! In the north Atlantic we did encounter bad storms. I was on deck on watch when a huge wave lifted part of the bomb-proof covering off one of the hatches and threw it against some rafts, which were smashed to bits and two men were swept overboard. In the lounge any furniture that had not been securely anchored to the floor was sent flying across the room. The tables had vertical rims (fiddles) and wet tablecloths to prevent things slipping off.

Our regular daily routine consisted of gym classes, boat and gun drill, attending lectures on first aid, gas, etc. Once in the Arctic Circle it got bitterly cold and we were all grateful for the warm clothing we had been donated before we left home. In all some two thousand four hundred volunteers were accepted. A few, sadly, were drowned on the way over and over two hundred died in action.

Wartime Memories Of A Gordon Highlander

I joined the Gordon Highlanders and did my initial training at their barracks in Aberdeen and later I was billeted in a modern glass clad school building there. This was not the safest place to be during the frequent lone aircraft raids that came in low over the sea to avoid detection but we did get a good view of the tracer bullets at night!

The bombs that did fall on Aberdeen sliced through the granite buildings making them resemble large open doll's houses! I spent the next three years training and going on manoeuvres all over Scotland and England. We were sent to the Orkney Islands to counter any possible attack by the Germans from occupied Norway. In Yorkshire we practiced crossings of the river Derwent, which is similar to the river Orne in Normandy and on the west coast of Scotland we practised wet and dry landings. Wherever I was stationed I found the local people (natives!) very hospitable – they would offer me meals they could ill afford to give me from their meagre rations. Fortunately I was able to give them food I received in food parcels from my parents in Argentina. In return I appreciated the hot baths they offered me in their homes!

During these years of the so-called 'Phoney War', I got regular leaves with rail passes to go wherever I chose; to my aunt and uncle near Warrington or friends all over Britain. In London I had the choice of staying at the Overseas Club, Canning House or BLAV house (British Latin American Volunteers) where I could be sure of meeting someone from Buenos Aires. Curiously I seldom saw any of my school friends, presumably because we had no common meeting place. On one occasion in London I was wearing my kilt, and my friend was wearing the maroon trews of his regiment, when a north American behind us said to his buddy "Say, look at those two! One with a skirt and the other in fancy pants!"

I was first posted to the 1st Battalion of the Gordons and rose to the rank of corporal. I was proud to have soldiers who had seen active service in France in my section. A year later I was selected as a candidate for officer training as I had been in my school cadet corps. So when the battalion was sent on leave prior to embarking for North Africa to join the 51st Highland Division in North Africa, I was taken off the draft. A short time later I was sent to OCTU (Officer Cadet Training Unit) in Heysham in Lancashire. My year in the ranks and experience on manoeuvres served me well to get through OCTU. On completion I was then posted to the 2nd Battalion of the Gordon Highlanders, and went on many manoeuvres in preparation for opening the second front in France. Field Marshal Montgomery, affectionately known as Monte by the troops, visited us standing on his jeep. We were paraded in an open square and he told us to break ranks so that he could see us and we could all see him!

Four of my younger brothers managed to come over to the UK when each reached nineteen years of age, and I managed to meet them all once or twice, although two joined the Indian Army and another was sent to the USA for flying training. Three of us saw active service in North Africa and/or France. Our mother was very brave and kept in touch with all of us. It was very sad that my brother in

PPA (Popski's Private Army), a commando unit, was killed at the end of the war in Italy. His Jeep ran over a mine on his return from reporting that a bridge over the River Po, in northern Italy, was passable.

Returning to my story, I first saw active service in Normandy with the 2nd Battalion of the Gordon Highlanders. It took three days to cross the English Channel in June 1944 during the worst storm for a hundred years which destroyed the American artificial Mulberry Harbour.

We landed on a low narrow wooden pier within the Mulberry harbour and were directed, surprisingly by a school friend, to go. We went to the nearest available field to dig a very shallow trench under cover of a hedgerow in which to sleep and waited for our much-delayed transport and hot food to arrive. We were part of the 15th Scottish Infantry Division which, together with the Guards Armoured Division and the Desert Rats Armoured Division, formed thirty Corps with a number of specialist units. Our job was to punch holes in the perimeter of the bridgehead, for which we became known as 'Montgomery's crowbar'. We then withdrew and handed over to a holding unit. This was repeated several times until the eventual break out. We witnessed the awesome sight of the thousand-bomber air raid above us, saw some planes shot down and crews parachuting to safety. We were then on the right of the line to protect the Americans who were coming south down the Cherbourg peninsular on the outside of the huge 'swing-door' centred on Falaise and preparing to make a dash for Paris.

Meanwhile we were also swinging round behind the Germans cutting off their retreat to the south and east and catching the enemy in a noose, known as the Falaise Gap, where the Germans lost most of their equipment and very many lives. Unfortunately, I became a casualty on the 6th August 1944 (early on in this offensive) in the small village of Estry, south of St. Lo. A mortar shell fell close to me and the shrapnel from it broke my jaw filling my mouth with bits of bone and loose teeth and I was unable to speak. I just remember being taken on a bren carrier, a small tracked vehicle, to a field hospital and having my mouth cleaned up. I was afraid to spit out the debris in my mouth as I had the sensation that I would loose part of myself forever! I was given a drink which promptly came out through a hole in my cheek! Thus I missed out on the chase across Northern France and Belgium to Germany. I was then flown to Britain to Park Prewett Hospital near Basingstoke. There I spent six months undergoing a series of operations to repair my cheek and replace my right jaw with a bone graft from my hip. I was fortunate to have the services of Sir Harold Gillies, the well-known pioneer plastic surgeon, for these operations. My jaws were wired up together so that I could only drink fluids with a straw though the gap in my lower jaw. Nurses from all the big London hospitals looked after us, each with their distinctive uniforms. We all got on well together and when feeling better used to tease the younger nurses, but not the matron! Between operations I was sent on leave to recuperate before returning to go on the 'slab' for the next operation.

January 1945 was reported to be the coldest for fifty years, so I was grateful for the woolly headgear, scarves and gloves sent by my parents in Argentina. In February I was posted to a holding unit in Ayr in South West Scotland where I was to stay until October doing light duties of pay and administration, including escorting drafts of soldiers and defending others charged with desertion and getting their sentences reduced to AWOL (although I had no legal training!)

April 23rd 1945 was a sad day. One brother was killed in Italy and another had just arrived from Argentina to volunteer for service in the British Army.

In May I took part in the VE Day parades and was able to meet one brother back from his flying training in the USA and the other who had recently arrived from Argentina. However I was preoccupied with my late brother's affairs. Another brother in the Indian Army in Italy contacted the farmers there who had buried my brother in a provisional grave by the roadside where he had been killed and later in the month I passed my medical board and was pronounced A1 fit again.

I was pleased to be posted back to my old unit, now returned from Germany, in October 1945 but there was no-one left there that I knew. I realized that being wounded had probably saved my life. We embarked on the 'Reina del Pacifico', converted to a large troop ship, bound for the Far East. I was lucky to get a double cabin, although I had to share it with fourteen others! We were in good company with QA nurses, ATS and VADs (not in our cabin though!)

When the war with Japan ended, we were off-loaded in Algiers and then Tripoli, in Libya, where our task was to

279

keep the peace between the Arab and Jewish desert tribes. We were billeted in ruined Italian barracks from colonial days, where the latrines were blocked and the doors and window frames removed for firewood. However we had a good time there visiting the extraordinary Roman remains, preserved by being covered by twenty feet of Sahara Desert sand. We were issued with dinghies with centreboards to sail between the wrecks in the harbour.

When the war ended we were demobbed in the order of the number given to us when we joined up to prevent mass unemployment by too many looking for jobs at the same time as happened at the end of World War One. As I had a comparatively high number, due to not being accepted for service until 1941, I was not due for demobbing for some time. So I applied for an accountancy course in Tel Aviv in the then British Palestine. This entailed going through Cairo, the Middle East HQ, where I took the opportunity to apply for early release on the grounds that I was applying for repatriation to Argentina and would therefore not do anyone out of a job in civvy street and be one less mouth to feed in the UK!

On my return through Cairo I was told that my request had been granted and on reaching my battalion in Tripoli was given twenty-four hours notice to catch a plane for Malta. There I waited a week to catch a boat to take me to Marseilles, from where a twenty-four hours train journey took me to Calais and the ferry across to the UK. I then had to report back to the Gordon Highlanders HQ in Aberdeen and was given leave until catching the 'Alcantara' in November 1946.

Wartime Memories Of A Gordon Highlander

On arrival in Buenos Aires, those under twenty-one years of age, regardless of rank, had to be claimed by their parents before being allowed to leave the ship! Welcome home parties were held for each ship of returned volunteers and at one of these I first met my future wife, Joan, who had travelled out on an earlier ship with one of my brothers without meeting each other! Thus ended my most interesting and varied war experiences on a very happy note.

I'd like to dedicate this account to my understanding and patient wife, Doreen.

A Window on My Life

As I Remember

By Don Taylor

During World War Two London was the German's nightly target. In June 1944 the 'V1' - a secret weapon nicknamed the 'Doodlebug' arrived. It was ingenious really; simply a jet engine attached to a flying bomb, which required no aircrew, and when it ran out of fuel – it dived and exploded.

On one particular night, the air-raid siren had sounded and later came the threatening throbbing sound of a doodlebug engine high up in the night sky. My mother and I were supposed to be sleeping in the Anderson Shelter at the bottom of our garden, but we were not asleep. It throbbed nearer and we were frightened as we lay listening. We prayed it would keep going, but it did not. Death had arrived on metal wings!

The V1 engine had stopped immediately overhead and then we heard a whistling sound getting closer, and frighteningly louder, as it dropped to earth. The jolt of the loud explosion then lifted me off the top bunk and threw me down to the floor while the small wooden door of the Anderson shelter was torn from its hinges and hit me on the head. I was stunned and my mother was screaming. Then the light went out and the air was thick with clouds of choking dust. We coughed and cuddled – but thankfully we were still alive. Then we heard a man's voice calling from somewhere outside; "Help! Will somebody help me?" "Don't leave me!" pleaded my mother. But the insistent voice outside was calling again. I could see the doorway was blocked with bricks, rubble and earth. We had been buried in the dark. I knew that the air within the Anderson Shelter would not last long but I said nothing to my mother who was already crying hysterically. Instinctively, I cuddled and tried to comfort her as best I could. My father and elder brother were serving in the forces so, at fifteen, I was the man of the house. I quickly began picking bricks and rubble out of the blocked doorway and, as luck would have it, suddenly saw a dim light and felt a cool rush of fresh air when I removed some of the bricks. Thankfully, I managed to clear enough bricks and rubble away so that I could climb out. "Don't leave me!" pleaded mum again, but the voice outside was calling more insistently. "I'm sorry, mum, but someone needs help," I said softly.

I climbed out of the shelter and saw that the top of our house had been blown away with rubble and devastation everywhere. Then I heard the man's voice calling again. I picked my way carefully through the assorted rubble and climbed across the back gardens towards where the voice was coming from. It was coming from upstairs in a neighbour's house, about four gardens away. The staircase of the house had been blown outside the shattered house, but it could still be climbed. Carefully, I climbed up the rickety, swaying staircase and what a sight I saw. All of the roof had been blown away and, from in the bedroom, I could see the stars in the sky. In this back bedroom was a naked man standing by his bed. He was covered from head to foot in thick black dust. He and his bed had been trapped as if in a huge wooden cage, hemmed in by all the long, fallen, ceiling joists. "Give me that suitcase from under the bed, son!" he said. I did as I was bid and he got dressed. Tersely, he thanked me.

A couple of significant things happened when that V1 exploded; the old night watchman who was in Boots the Chemist in Green Street, Upton Park was killed and, within ten minutes of the explosion, all the suits were stolen from the fifty bob tailor's shop which had all its windows broken by the V1! Unfortunately, thieves are always with us.

Anyway, this is how I remember one night about sixty-two years ago - when I was just a fresh faced young lad.

A Window on My Life

The Evacuees

By Don MacKenzie

Born in the East End of London during the Depression year of 1931, Don Mackie was the love child of Len and Maude. Unfortunately for them, Don was conceived outside of wedlock. In order to hide their shame, the couple got married very hastily and, after the baby was born, Maude was to insist her baby boy had been two months premature. As a child, Maude was found to have an enlarged heart and, soon after Don was born, she was advised against having any more children. However, in spite of this warning, Don was to be joined by a baby brother eighteen months later. Because of Maude's heart condition, she had to stay in the hospital for quite some time after the birth so Don was fostered out to an aunt.

The Depression was still going on all around and Len was still without work. The family had very little money to spend on any kind of luxury, let alone paying out for any kind of birth control. Because of this situation, and in spite of all the warnings, Maude had yet another baby but this time it was to be a girl. While Maude spent more time in the hospital recovering, Don and his brother were fostered out once again.

As soon as the family were all reunited, they had something else to celebrate. They were given a house on a council estate just outside London. The only unfortunate thing about this new situation was that Len had to cycle eleven miles back into London in order to sign on at the Labour Exchange. This he had to do twice each day in order that he could collect the meagre amount of money given to feed his family.

It was now late in 1935. Len was still without work along with thousands of other men, who all had to live on State handouts. Although very poor, the family was very happy and, in February 1936, Maude gave birth to another girl.

The following year, Maude fell pregnant again. It was another boy but, this time, the baby lived for only ten months. Again, in 1938, Maude was once again giving birth and this time she delivered twins. Within a few hours they were both dead. Maude was now very ill, her heart condition did not allow for the workload her body was giving it. She was now having many operations on her heart to keep her alive. Because of her continued stay in hospital, all three children were fostered out. The two boys stayed together with their sister going to another family.

The family that Don and his brother were living with were old friends of the family and, over the following years, Don was to be taken in by this family many times. In fact, the boys didn't mind going there at all. The lady of the house became Don's favourite aunt and Don also liked the fact that one of her daughters was around his own age.

It was now the summer of 1939. There was talk of war with Germany. It was to be the turning point in so many peoples' lives. Thoughts were going back to the previous war with Germany.

The Evacuees

In the September of this year war was declared. Don and his brother were evacuated to a small village in Somerset called Norton Fitz Warren. The village was considered far enough away for the German bombers not to reach. The Evacuation Day began like any other day; the boys left home and went to school as normal but, unusually, were accompanied by their mother on this occasion.

Once at school, each child had their name-tag attached to their coat and all were given a gas mask in a box to be slung around their neck. Maude gave Don an extra parcel to carry with orders to give it to whoever they were going to stay with. Then, suddenly, all the children were asked to board the buses that were waiting outside the school and there were many tears as each child was kissed goodbye by their parents. Don and his brother were no exception. They both hugged their mother and then boarded the bus. Within an hour, all the children were boarding a train and, after the train pulled out, they were on their way.

At this point, the evacuation started to be very exciting; it was like going to the seaside. After what seemed like a whole day travelling, the children finally reached their destination. From the train, they were all taken to the local school and told to sit down. Once all the children were seated, people started to walk among them and it was as if the children were cattle in a market awaiting a buyer. Don started to realise that the children were being looked over and selected as evacuees by the local population. He and his brother just sat there awaiting their turn to be picked and, after what seemed like ages, the number of children dwindled down to about a dozen.

Suddenly, a young girl beckoned Don and his brother over; she looked about thirteen or fourteen and standing at her side were two other boys she had already selected. All four boys were then asked to follow her and she lead them to where a man was seated at a table. After taking the boys' names and other particulars the man looked at the boys and said, "Okay boys, I want you to go with Mandy and she will take you home to her parents." All four boys did as they were told. Following Mandy, they walked about a quarter of a mile and were then lead down some steps into a garden before walking up a path to a big house. As soon as they were inside, they were greeted by four adults - two of them being Mandy's parents and another couple who appeared to be in their early twenties and were renting part of the house from Mandy's parents.

Almost immediately, the four boys were parted with Don and his brother being lead into another part of the house by the young couple. Both boys were asked to sit down at a prepared table to eat a meal. After sitting down, Don decided to hand over the small parcel from his mother that he'd been carrying around all day. He had no idea what was inside but the lady took it from him and said "thankyou". Inside was a short note from the boy's mother and a few tins of food to help out given the rationing. After their meal, the boys were asked quite a few questions about their lives and what was going on in London.

It was now early evening and the couple decided that the boys should have an early night after such an arduous day. The young lady then led them up two flights of stairs and into a bedroom. The two brothers were quite surprised to see the other two boys in the room and already tucked up in bed – there was only one bed in the room and it was a mattress on the floor. Don and his young brother were told to undress and get into the bed alongside the other two boys.

All four boys were assured that the sleeping arrangements were for one night only and that they would have their own beds the following night. After saying their 'good nights', the four adults went out of the room shutting the door behind them. The boys just lay there in silence when, suddenly, the younger of the other two brothers started to cry. Within a matter of minutes, all four boys were bawling their eyes out and calling out for their parents. During the whole time the boys were crying, not once did any of the adults come in to comfort them but, eventually, all four dropped off to sleep with sheer exhaustion.

The next day, the boys were shown over the house and to their new bedroom on the third floor. This bedroom was also the attic with just one bed but the bed was big enough for two small boys. The only other furniture was a small dressing table. The room was dark and the only daylight came from a small window in the roof and it was much too high for the boys to look out from. The other two boys occupied the same room that they had slept in the previous night. Mandy had a room of her own adjacent to the boys on the second floor, but Don never did discover where all the adults slept. Because of the large increase of children in the village, the hours for schooling were greatly reduced.

This resulted in the four boys having to go into school mornings only. They couldn't have been more delighted as it gave them more time to explore the countryside. Coming from the bricks and mortar of London this was all a great new venture. They had never seen so many animals in their short lives and there was no more crying for home - in fact, they were to enjoy living life to the very full.

My Life Story

By Peggy Miller

I was born in Thundersley, Essex and contracted polio when I was nearly two years old.

I started school at Rushbottom Lane School at the age of only 3? because I cried to go with my elder sister. It was a small school with only three classrooms and an old-fashioned black stove in the corner of the room which was our only form of heating. Rushbottom Lane School was the only school in that road then - now there are three!

In 1940, when I was eleven years old, I was evacuated to Mansfield Woodhouse which is about twenty miles from Nottingham. I lived with a married couple and, like most evacuees, I was 'put upon'. I had to carry buckets of coal even though I had Plaster of Paris on my legs too help straighten them. How I managed I will never know.

My mother visited me in the August after I had been staying there for about three months and decided to stay - she found a job as a housekeeper to a retired miner. He used to work above the pit and we had a happy 3? years there.

A few months later, in the January, my sister Joyce joined us. Every Saturday night we would all go to the pictures and my mum used to take her knitting to do in the interval (back then you watched two films with an interval in-between). One night we were sitting right at the back of the cinema and, in the interval, she duly got out her knitting and started to knit. Unfortunately, this particular night, she

293

dropped the ball of wool she was knitting with and it rolled from the back of the cinema where we were sitting, through the seats, and right to the front. It took her ages to pull it back and re-wind it all and I think she was more careful after that!

In 1951 I went to a Government Training School for the disabled in Letchworth, Hertfordshire to learn shorthand and typing and it was there that I had my first invalid car. One of the other students accompanied me and taught me to drive. The first time I went out by myself, however, I turned it over! Luckily I was unhurt and taken to the village police station (which was really the front room of a house) where I waited until someone came to collect me. As I had finished my course, I had to take a job until the car was repaired and I could return home again.

Once I thought I had broken down as the car wouldn't start and a passing car towed me home (about 2 miles) but when I got home I realised that I hadn't switched the petrol on!

Since then, I have had ordinary cars but gave up driving when I started getting arthritis in my shoulders and couldn't turn the wheel. Another time, I was coming home from Chelmsford and took the wrong turning and ended up in Danbury! Here ends the tale of my little escapades!